PARENTS' GUIDE TO TEENAGER ANXIETY AND DEPRESSION

THE MUST-HAVE GUIDE FOR UNDERSTANDING AND HELPING YOUR TEENAGER BATTLE ANXIETY AND DEPRESSION

S.L. CLARK

CONTENTS

If you take care of your mind, you take care of the world.

— ARIANNA HUFFINGTON

INTRODUCTION

As your child grows up, it's only natural that they pull away from you and explore their independence as they become their own person. However, it's understandable that they'll face obstacles on this journey. Sitting back feels unnatural, but teens need to make their own choices—and mistakes—to find out who they truly are.

In some cases, though, parents shouldn't just sit back and watch. It can be hard to tell when to be a silent supporter or when you need to step in and help your teen stay on the right path. Knowing the signs of anxiety and depression empower you to see when your teenager is suffering. It gives you the knowledge necessary to get them through tough times without detrimental side effects.

Since teens experience such a roller coaster of emotions, it's common for adults to disregard anything a teen claims is a struggle. However, anxiety and depression aren't related to hormonal mood swings, and they are not phases. These are mental conditions that can have long-lasting, negative effects on teens.

It's common to experience anxiety before an exam or presentation, but if your teen seems anxious for two weeks or longer, it could be a more severe type of anxiety. They might have panic attacks that suddenly spring up on them and make them fear something they were never worried about before. They might feel like they don't fit in with their peers and allow this worry to hinder their daily life. Though most teens are anxious about the future, if your teen lets this worry cripple them, then they are experiencing anxiety.

The stereotype of depression is someone who can't get out of bed, doesn't shower for days on end, and won't leave the house. However, that's an extreme view. Depression in teens looks different. Many teens know that they have to get up and go to school or face severe consequences, so they push themselves to get through each day. Yet depression can present emotionally, when they are irritable about every-thing, can't handle stress, or aren't interested in hobbies and subjects they used to love.

Watching your teen struggle is heartbreaking. If you're unsure of when and how to help your teen, then this book is for you. You'll learn about anxiety and depression and how they present in teens. You'll understand what these emotional and mental situations feel like to your teen as well as what negative behaviors they can lead to. Having this foundation of knowledge tells you what to look for.

Most importantly, you'll learn how you can help your teen during these times. You'll get actionable tips for talking to them, relating to them, and inspiring them to open up to you.

As a father of two, I understand the delicate balance of letting your children explore their boundaries and teaching them lessons you learned the hard way. Adults often remember their teenage years from a distance, not really recalling the range of strong emotions you could feel in one day. It's okay to not remember all of that because things are different now. Teenagers these days are experiencing things us as parents didn't have to think about at their ages.

There was no social media where you were encouraged to show off your life—whether it was reality or not. That meant there was also one less outlet for bullying. Kids these days can never completely get a break from their peers because social media and cell phones give them the opportunity to stay connected 24/7.

Social media is supposed to be fun and lighthearted, but it doesn't seem that way for teens. Understanding the implications of what they are posting and sharing is important for them—and you. Instead of guessing at what's going on, this book guides you through navigating this issue, and many more, with your teen.

When you have children going through the teen years, they aren't the only ones experiencing turmoil. It's tough for parents, too, so learning how to create a healthy, happy home is key for all family members, regardless of age. An entire chapter is dedicated to this concept. A happy home is crucial for your teen; you want them to feel safe and secure. Providing them with this solid foundation gives them a leg up on other kids who don't have everything you can provide —all while encouraging your teens to have empathy and understanding of the world around them.

I'm passionate about mental health and have researched it extensively for my own health as well as that of my two children. I understand how it feels to watch your teen struggle while you're unsure about how to help. I've been there, floundering and debating if I should step in or let them learn on their own. I've put all of my experience, knowledge, and research into this book, so you don't have to feel that uncertainty.

This book is made to be read straight through or used as a reference guide. If you're having specific troubles with your teen and social media, for example, you can jump right to Chapter 3 for information you can immediately put into action.

If you're reading this as a parent of a younger child or preteen, you might prefer to read it all the way through, so you're prepared for things that will come your way in the next few years. Even if you haven't noticed any signs of anxiety and depression in your child, this book can help you know what to look for and how to address it when you see it.

Each chapter is full of information on a certain topic. It opens with general knowledge, so you're acclimated to the subject before doing a deep dive. This is where I present my research and share resources that you can easily implement in your own parenting. Finally, each chapter ends with a summary. The bullet points reiterate the most important information, so you can refer back to them as needed.

There are some things that are difficult to navigate, like the changing political and social climate and, of course, the pandemic. While these issues hopefully won't continue being such toxic topics for teens, it's important to understand them and know how to talk about them with your teen. Therefore, while the research in this book is timeless, there are references to the pandemic and lockdown since those are still relevant issues.

The landscape of what teenagers have to deal with is constantly changing, but the foundation stays the same. If you want to give your teen a strong foundation of support, this book is for you. If you're ready to be a rock for your teen and really understand what they are going through instead of offering empty words of support, this book empowers you to do so.

When you apply the research in this book to your own life, you'll be amazed at how adept you feel in handling your teen's struggles. Your teen will also benefit by realizing you truly do understand what they are going through. They'll see that you're there for them—willing to research and do the work to help them make the most of their life.

1

INTO THE MIND OF A TEEN

E ach generation is different from the one that came before. They are raised differently, have different interests and values, and will accomplish different things in their futures. Not only are the people of each generation— baby boomers, millennials, and Gen Z—drastically unique but so is the world in which they live.

Baby boomers grew up without most of the technology that millennials had—even though that rapidly progressed throughout their lives as well. Now, Gen Z has access to the world at their fingertips. They can get in touch with anyone, anywhere, and at any time. There are no limits, so it's up to you, as parents, to set those limits.

Parenting is tough enough in what people now think of as "normal" times, but with the changing political and social climate, not to mention the pandemic and lockdown, everyone is facing a unique situation. There's no guidebook for how to keep your children safe, occupied, and educated when you're stuck in your house. Parents have struggled with educating and raising their kids while also working from home, trying to keep everyone sane and optimistic. It's a tall order, but you don't have to know all of the answers.

If you have a foundation of knowledge about the teenage years, you'll feel better equipped to roll with the punches. Understanding the signs of anxiety and depression can keep you attuned to your teen whether they are sitting at the kitchen table in virtual school or getting off the school bus at the end of the day.

THE MODERN TEEN VS. THE OLD TEEN

Naming generations and assigning broad characteristics to that demographic isn't a new phenomenon. Social scientists have roughly defined periods for generations going back to the 1900s (Cottrell, 2020). A generation usually encompasses a 20-year period. Since the people born in this time go through many of the same cultural and historical events, they have similar life experiences and can relate to each other. However, that doesn't mean that people born in the same generation experienced everything the same way. Millennials, for example, could have been anywhere from kindergarten to college during the September 11th terrorist attacks. A college freshman living in the New York University dorms would have drastically different memories than a kindergartener in California.

Still, living through major events like that bonds people in a way, so scientists agree that 20 years isn't too broad for a generation. A generation typically spans between 20 to 30 years, since that's when people reach adulthood and begin having their own children (International Society of Genetic Genealogy, 2016).

The Greatest Generation was born between 1901 and 1924. They experienced the Great Depression and fought in World War II. The Silent Generation was born between 1928 and 1945. This name came about because they stayed silent as Communism took over the country. Both of these generations are thought of as being strict parents who valued work ethic more than relating to their children on an emotional level.

Baby boomers were born between 1946 and 1964. When the Greatest Generation came home from World War II, they started families at a high rate, causing a baby boom. This is the first generation that talked to their children, popularizing family meetings and trying to understand what their children were going through.

Generation X consists of people born between 1965 and 1980. Society majorly changed during this time with landmark events like the AIDS epidemic, LGBTQIA+ awareness, and an influx of home technology. This is stereotypically thought of as the slacker generation, though after having families of their own, they are thought of as the first helicopter parents.

Millennials were born between 1981 and 1996. In addition to the previously mentioned 9/11 terrorist attacks, millennials also lived through war and terrorism for many years following that event. Most people from this generation grew up with the Internet, which started changing their lives and approach to work and social situations. This is the first generation that had easy access to a lot of technology.

As parents, millennials are well-rounded and open-minded. They've experienced a lot due to the connectivity of the Internet and are sharing this knowledge and acceptance with their children. This leads to their children, Gen Z, feeling free to express who they really are. Some millennials may have had helicopter Generation X parents, so they are staying away from this and giving their children more space to learn from their mistakes.

Who Are the iGens or Gen Z?

Gen Z consists of people born from 1997 to 2012. It's also known as the iGen, a play on words referring to the popularity of Apple products, such as the iPhone, iPod, iPad, iMac, and so on. Though this generation has access to more technology than any that came before them, it doesn't mean they are lazy or entitled. In fact, many iGens have taken advantage of this connectivity to make huge strides in social justice and activism.

Social scientists have identified children born in 2010 and later as Generation Alpha (Pasquarelli & Schultz, 2019). This generation is reaching preteen years, so whether you have an iGen or Generation Alpha, it's important to pay attention to the knowledge shared in this book. Understanding the approach to depression and anxiety will give you a solid foundation for parenting—even if social media and technology changes as your Alpha reaches teenage years and young adulthood.

What Are the Differences?

This generation has only known constant internet access. As young children, they most likely played educational games on tablets or watched a show on a parent's phone when they were bored in public. Now, this generation has reached preteen and teenage years and are more tech-savvy than anyone who came before them.

This technical know-how is a great thing in terms of marketable skills. Many millennial parents might remember their own guardians struggling to master typing and computer skills to stay relevant in the job market. So knowing that your children are learning these skills naturally can be a relief, especially if they are able to help you troubleshoot your own devices.

But there's such a thing as overexposure to technology, social media, and the Internet. It provides a disconnect that prevents many teens from realizing that they are talking to real people online. When you're behind a screen, you might feel more confident in what you say, which can help teens explore their true selves... or make them meaner to who they are interacting with. It's easier to disagree with someone and call them names when you don't have to see the hurt in their eyes.

Similarly, it's easy to post pictures and personal information when you don't realize the scope of your audience. Teens often feel like the most important person in the world and the most protected at the same time. While it's true that their world revolves around themselves, putting things on the Internet opens them up to anyone and everyone around the world. You'll learn more about the importance of privacy and internet safety in "Chapter 3: The Online Environment of New Teens."

Not all internet use is a bad thing. Since iGens have a broader reach, they are likely to have friends in other countries and learn about those cultures. They feel connected to a broader range of people compared to generations that were limited to friends in their neighborhood or parents' social circles.

The Internet can also benefit teens because they have more resources. They don't have to go to the library to find an encyclopedia or try to start a club that encompasses their interests. The Internet provides this for them. As a result, they can research more on their own and get more involved with hobbies and causes that are important to them. This gives them the capability to be more knowledgeable, less entitled, more confident, and less likely to sit back and let the world happen around them.

WHAT GOES ON IN THEIR MIND?

Understanding when iGens were born and what's important to them gives you a solid foundation to start understanding them. If you know what goes on in their mind, you'll be in a better position to know what they are feeling, and the signs of depression and anxiety will become clear to you.

The teenage years are always a struggle. Think of your own adolescent period and highlight three of your strongest memories. They most likely have to do with love, anger, or excitement. Maybe you remember your first relationship and subsequent heartbreak; a huge blowout you had with your parents when you told them your plans after high school graduation; or maybe you remember the elation you felt as you took off your graduation cap and tossed it in the air along with your classmates.

Most people remember the highs and lows, but that's not just because the extreme emotions stand out to you more. It's because so much of your teenage years revolve around extreme emotions. When you're a teenager, your hormones are changing drastically, making it hard to have logical reactions to things. Your body physically won't let you stay calm and even-keeled because it's going through so much at once.

Yet remembering the emotions you went through years ago doesn't necessarily give you a better understanding of your teen. Their environment is different. They are going through different things in their mind, but the world around them is also drastically different than it was when you were a teen. Think of the news stories and political debates from your teen years, and compare them to now. You most likely went to school every day, while teens recently adapted to virtual schooling at home or in other environments that weren't their usual classrooms. They've experienced a major upheaval in the past few years as politics and social justice take on more importance than ever before.

A basic understanding of the teenage brain and the changes it's undergoing during these years gives you a foundation of knowledge. You'll know the biological information that affects their thoughts and emotions. Then, you can overlay any social, political, or medical turmoil that might be going on in the world around them.

Understanding the Brain

Teens feel like they are grown up just because they are experiencing more independence as they get older, but in reality, their brain isn't fully developed until they are closer to 25 (Ramunda, 2018). They might think they know what's best for them, but their brain is closer to that of a child. This difference is obvious if you look at the brain using magnetic imagining, which shows that it's physically not as large as an adult's brain.

During childhood, the brain learns at an exponential rate, making connections as kids explore the world around them, ask questions, and learn the answers. They easily learn new things throughout their teenage and college years, too, until the brain is fully developed in their mid-20s.

When you think back to your teenage and college years, you can probably pinpoint some bad decisions that seemed like good ideas at the time. That's what your teen is experiencing now. They feel like they have all of the information needed to make a good choice, but they don't have the life experience to actually know if the decision is a good one. Therefore, this maturity isn't just related to brain development but also to experience and understanding consequences.

Teenagers also don't have a fully developed frontal lobe. This part of the brain is responsible for attention spans and impulse control. It won't fully develop until your teen is well into their 20s. Since the frontal lobe is still developing, teens most likely make impulsive decisions based on emotions alone, centering from their amygdala. The amygdala controls anger, fear, and panic. Therefore, their decisions are based on what seems right for the immediate future. They are making a snap decision just to get it done, but they are not processing the issue and making a choice depending on potential long-term consequences.

Since so much of their thinking takes place in the amygdala, your teen also has trouble interpreting emotions. If you're talking to them about their report card, they can't listen to what you're saying and rationally realize that you're encouraging them to do better. Instead, they interpret what you're saying as disappointment or scolding and immediately feel dejected or depressed.

When your teen is experiencing strong emotions, that's the only thing they can focus on. Everything else they are seeing, hearing, and feeling—if anything is getting through—is filtered through this emotion. Therefore, things that should be minor issues might feel more severe. Happy moments might be tinged with sadness because your teen can't separate everything yet. They feel completely immersed in their emotions.

You might think that your teen being so focused on their emotions means that they are incapable of hearing or learning other things, but that's not true. Just because your teen's brain isn't as mature as an adult's doesn't mean they can't handle certain information. During the teen years, their brains are actually especially receptive to learning new things and exploring their limits (Clarkson, 2017).

Teens are impulsive because of the dopamine production as their hormones change. They get hooked on the feeling of exhilaration after doing something tough or wild, so they want to do more of that to feel dopamine. As they mature, their body will regulate dopamine more, and your teen will learn to control themselves.

Dopamine and the increased production of other hormones make teens more at risk for addiction. You'll learn more about this in Chapter 5, but it's important to know that most addictions during the teen years are a result of hormones. It can be tempting to blame your teen for bad behavior and restrict their access to friends, outings, and other privileges, but knowing that hormones are at the root gives you a better understanding of what they are going through.

Due to the impulsivity and addiction to dopamine, at the very least, teens are likely to ignore consequences. They feel immortal, like nothing can hurt them, and like they'll never get in trouble for any behavior. They are not mature enough to understand about things they do catching up to them in one way or another. Therefore, they are more likely to make poor choices because they don't understand possible consequences and don't think any will affect them. They want the impulsive action, the dopamine hit, and the thrill of doing something more than they want to worry about what might come next.

All of these issues stem from brain chemistry. Your teen will grow out of them as their brain matures, but understanding this issue while they are experiencing it is a great source of support for them. You know not to scold your teen directly but rather approach them from a place of understanding to show them that you relate to them. Teens always think their parents haven't gone through what they are currently experiencing, but knowing about brain chemistry and hormones will help both parents and teens.

How to Combat This Problem

Giving your teen an outlet can help them manage their feelings. If you show them that you're available to talk, they'll be more likely to come to you with even minor problems. Listen with an open mind and don't disregard their feelings. Don't ask them to push their feelings aside and focus on the cold hard facts. Just be there to be their sounding board.

Since they are so emotional and rely so much on their amygdala, it can be hard to communicate with teens. What you're saying often gets distorted by what they are feeling, so emotions get in the way and build up barriers. Knowing that your teen is emotional during these years can help you think about what you're saying and adjust your tone before you talk to them.

It's also important to sit with them and really talk to ensure they hear what you're saying, and you understand their reactions. Prioritizing conversations like this helps teens realize what you're truly saying and creates a strong foundation of trust that is crucial to implement what you'll learn from this book.

That being said, you still want to give teens their space. You don't want them to feel like you're nosy, always trying to get in their business to judge them or restrict their freedoms. If you show them that you're open to conversations whenever they need you, they are more likely to come to you on their own. When they feel like you're receptive to what they have to say, they'll naturally want to share more with you.

It can be difficult, but you want to give teens a chance to make their own mistakes. They'll learn better through their own trial and error instead of you preventing them from trying anything in the first place. You might know that it's a bad idea for them to try and dye their hair neon green because you ruined your own at their age, but they are not going to care about that. They want to do it anyway, so you have to let them.

There are some obvious instances when you need to step in and be a strict parent, but you'll learn more about those times in the chapters about the detrimental effects of depression and anxiety. You'll also learn to tell the difference between the emotional ups and downs of a typical teen compared to the more severe impact of depression and anxiety.

IN SUMMARY

Understanding teenagers' generations is just as important as knowing how their brains work.

- Generations encompass 20 to 30 years. People raised in this time have similar shared experiences, especially regarding technology and historical and social events.
- Teenagers are emotional—not only because of their changing hormones but because their brains are still developing. They won't have an adult brain until they are 25 years old.
- The changing brain and body chemistry make teens emotional in their decisions and reactions. They take in information and speak or act out without stopping and thinking logically about the situation. It isn't personal; it's just how they function while they are going through puberty and maturing.
- Understanding your teen's brain—and the fact that their emotions are leading the way—will help you have a better relationship with them. Be open to their conversation and have patience even when it seems like they are not listening or getting carried away with their emotions.
- Initiate conversations with your teen—even if it seems like they don't want to talk. Don't push the issue, but make sure they know you're always there for them. Being a parent means you're the one in charge. Learn more about your roles in the next chapter.

2

WHAT'S YOUR ROLE?

There are parents who say they want to be their kid's best friend, and there are parents that rule with strictness. The truth is that parenthood is something of a balance between the two. Being too friendly with your teen means they won't respect your boundaries. They'll think they are free to do what they want and act like an adult—or what they think an adult acts like.

On the other hand, being too strict pushes your child away from you. They feel like they'll get in trouble for even the smallest infraction, so they might as well do something really bad to make their punishment worth it.

Knowing your role as a parent is understanding how to relate to your teen while setting healthy boundaries. It's your job to give your teen a safe, healthy, and happy house as their launchpad. You're teaching them how to be a good person—both in your words and with your example. But you're also letting them explore their own life and own boundaries. You want to empower them to make choices, so they understand decision-making and the resulting consequences.

THE ROLE OF A PARENT IN A TEEN'S LIFE

You might not realize it when you and your teen have a big blowout argument, but your teen loves you. They treasure you for all you provide for them. You keep a roof over their head and food on the table. You buy them clothes—even if you make them spend their own money on the trendy items they seem to favor one day and hate the next. You're giving them a solid foundation and healthy boundaries where they can be both your child and their own selves.

When you support your teen through the good times and the bad, you're showing them that they can rely on you. You're there, always, without judgment. You're there to help when they need it and to comfort them when they are upset. They see this every day. They know they can come to you, and they will when they need you. By always being present, they'll know you're available any time.

What a Parent Must Do

Parenting classes don't prepare you for the reality of raising a child, and parenting a younger child doesn't even give you an idea of what to expect when they hit the preteen years. There's no way of knowing exactly what's necessary to raise another person until you're in the thick of it. By then, you're learning as you go. These guidelines help you understand what a parent must do. They are broad and give general examples because everyone's life is different. You'll most likely see yourself in these qualities, though. Seeing that you're on the right path gives you what's needed to push ahead and continue creating this healthy foundation for your teen's life.

Teach by Example

From early childhood, parents teach their children about society. When you quiet your child's tantrum in the grocery store, you're giving them clues on how to act in public. When you go to the corner, press the "walk" button, and wait for the lights to direct you into the crosswalk, you're teaching them the rules, as well as safety. You might explain these lessons to them the first time or two, but after that, you're leading by example. And your child is picking up on that. You're their first teacher—the one they learn the most from over the entire course of their life.

By teaching them these broad guidelines of society at a young age, you're giving them a framework. You're telling them what the public expects while also giving them the freedom to become themselves. When you're teaching your child these rules, you're showing them how to keep society running smoothly. If everyone follows this basic foundation of kindness and compassion, then the world is safer for all involved.

Of course, life doesn't work that way. People jaywalk and, when teaching your teen to drive, you have to adjust these rules and explain to them that everyone doesn't use the crosswalk and follow the lights. However, you're instilling a sense of what's right and wrong in your child from the very first time you crossed the street at the corner. They'll remember that and internalize it. That doesn't mean they feel the need to bad-mouth anyone who jaywalks, but they'll understand the differences between the two approaches.

When you teach your child how to act in public, these general ideas will evolve as your child matures. They'll use this information to interact with teachers and classmates in school. By the time they are a teenager applying to their first job, they'll know how to greet the interviewer and how to politely shake hands. This knowledge will evolve as they enter college and the professional job market, as well as apply to their social situations along the way.

Be a Role Model

Your children learn all of this from you simply because you're their role model. Since they are already looking at you for cues about how to behave in society, it's only natural that they look at you for information about moral behavior as well.

When your teen acts a certain way or makes a decision, they are going to look at you for approval. Approval doesn't mean you're telling them they did the right thing. You don't have to say a word because your teen can tell that they've done the same thing you would. That means you were a role model for them when they were younger to the extent that they already know what you'd do in their shoes.

Being a role model for your teen doesn't mean you have to be perfect, and neither do they. In fact, showing your teen that adults make mistakes will help them feel more comfortable opening up to you. If you try to act like you've never had a problem or said or done the wrong thing, your teen won't feel like they can relate to you. They'll look at themselves and think they are flawed compared to you. They won't think you understand what they are struggling with, so they'll keep it all to themselves.

Think back to when you were a teenager. You probably thought adults had it all together. Once you graduated college and got a job, it'd be smooth sailing because adulthood was the end of your problems. Now, as an adult and a parent, you know better than anyone that it's not true. Everyone experiences ups and downs throughout their entire life. Things don't get easier just because you reach a certain age.

Your teen probably still thinks your life is flawless. Talking openly with your teen shows them that you have problems in your life, too. They'll not only get a realistic view of adulthood, but they'll be able to relate to you better. Your teen will know they can come to you with friendship problems because you've had similar troubles recently. They'll talk to you about classmates at school because you share information about your job and co-workers.

As a parent, you don't have to make everything seem perfect. You can be yourself with your teen and share your life with them as you want them to share their life with you. After all, you're their role model, and this is one of the most important things you want them to imitate from you.

Set Limits and Boundaries

When you're a new parent, it's understood that you take complete care of your child. You buckle them into the car seat and drive carefully. You hold their hand in parking lots. You take care of them when they are sick. They are so young that they are not able to do any of that for themselves.

As your kid grows up and hits the teenage years, they'll think they know everything. They gripe at you when you remind them to buckle their seat belt. They don't want to hold your hand anymore. When they are sick, they want to be left alone. It can hurt when your teen reaches this stage because you're accustomed to taking care of them. It's been your main job for so long that now you feel like you're being pushed away.

Your teen thinking they don't need you at this point is actually a good thing. You've raised them to know how to be independent, take care of themselves, and look out for harm. Yet that doesn't mean they are always going to follow these guidelines.

As you learned, teen brains are highly emotional. Your teen might know to buckle up and look both ways before crossing the street, but they might still push those boundaries. It can be worrying to see them acting this way, but it's a normal part of the teen experience. They are testing the limits. As long as they stay safe and know the rules, you can let your teen explore in this way. But you don't always have to be this way. You can be flexible when needed, or get strict when they are putting themselves in danger.

If you created boundaries from childhood, you would feel confident that your teen knows the rules and has those limits ingrained in their personality. If you didn't establish this type of boundary when your child was young, it's not too late. When you're working to show your teen that you're a role model creating a healthy home environment for them, you can lay some ground rules. Tell them what is and isn't acceptable behavior for you. Discuss the limits and what consequences they'll face if they break your trust. Once all of the rules are out in the open, you can feel assured that your teen at least knows the boundaries, though they'll likely still test them.

Teach Decision-Making Skills

You know that the teen brain is highly emotional. They don't pause to think things through, instead reacting to whatever information they are faced with. This means it's important for parents to help teens learn decision-making skills. They'll learn how to do this on their own, in time, but you can help them while they wait for their brain to mature.

As parents, you've lived a longer life and experienced more things than your teen. You aren't just reacting to anything that is said or done to you. You're pausing, taking it in, and looking over your past experiences for related events. You're pulling from your knowledge to react accordingly. You can do this, to an extent, for your teen as well. You don't have to tell them exactly what you've been through, and you don't need to make the decision for them, but you can give them the steps they should take to make a decision, and you can help guide them as they practice it for themselves.

To practice the decision-making steps, you can either use something your teen is going through, if they confided in you, or make up a situation. Have them tell you what's going on in their life or a story that interests them. Find the problem and ask questions to get the details needed, so you can give them accurate guidance. They might think they are having trouble with a friend because of how the friend is acting, but maybe it's something in the way your teen is treating them or in the friend's home life. It's easy to think that the problem is surface-level, but you often have to dig deeper than that. Pinpointing the specific problem will prepare your teen for understanding how to make real-life choices.

Your guidance shouldn't be heavy-handed. You should use this as a teaching moment to tell your teen how they should work their way through the problem. Sometimes, the answer is crystal clear, but sometimes, it takes many steps and a lot of time to get past. Even in the case of natural consequences helping them through a decision, guidance can help prepare them for that possibility. At this stage, you're teaching them how to cover their bases and think of all outcomes.

Guidance will get your teen on the right path to think of several different options to solve the problem. They might think there's only one or two ways to get past it because they don't have much experience. You can help them understand how to approach a problem from a different angle. You can tell them to take some time away, and when they think about it again, they might see something they hadn't realized before. You can even write a list of outcome options to keep everything organized. Sometimes, seeing the solutions on paper will help your teen understand them in a different way or think of something else.

After thinking of different solutions and picking the right one, your teen can make a path forward. Again, they might want to write out the steps, so they see what they are going to have to do. Talking and writing things out also helps your teen realize that decision-making doesn't happen with a snap of their fingers. They have to devote time to the issue and really think about the possible paths before taking action.

Decision-making doesn't only relate to things your teen is experiencing in their daily life; it can also result from questions. Many parents get tired of hearing questions from their child and teen. They wonder about some of the strangest things, like how the whale got to be so large or if you'd rather eat a worm or a squirrel. It's tempting to wave these questions away, but they are a great opportunity for learning and togetherness.

In terms of questions like how a whale got so large, you can do research. Look up some facts together. You can use this opportunity to show your child what online resources are available and are reputable sources. Again, this is being a role model and modeling the behavior you'd like them to learn. You don't simply type in the question and take the first search engine result as the truth. You do a little digging, find a factual site, and learn from there. Taking time to go online with your child in response to questions like this can help them have a healthy relationship with social media later. You'll learn more about that in the next chapter.

When they ask you silly questions, there's no harm in answering—even if you're otherwise occupied. You can also turn the question around and ask them. When they answer, ask them why they chose that answer. Make them think about what they are saying. Help them find logic in their decision. Making time to talk with them like this will help them with decision-making as they grow older. Plus, you're showing them that they can come to you, and you're available to talk and listen.

As your child matures into a teen, their questions might become more philosophical and deeper. They'll ask about their body, love, religion, death, and more. Since you took time to help them find answers as a child, they are comfortable coming to you now. Helping them find answers to deeper questions, and talking about the information you find, will help their decision-making skills. They know how to formulate a question, think about it themselves, and then find out an answer from a trustworthy source.

Provide Emotional Support

Providing emotional support means that you're always available when you're needed. This can be hard to provide sometimes because teens rarely come to their parents on their own. They might sulk in their room after a bad day or stay silent at dinner—even when you're asking them questions.

When you provide emotional support to your younger child —by comforting them when they are scared; applying bandages when they are hurt; and helping them learn the big things, like how to walk, roller-skate, ride a bike, and more— they already see you as a source of emotional support. This will continue when they are a teen—even if you feel like they've completely closed you out.

If your teen doesn't respond to questions or won't tell you when something's wrong, you don't have to sit back and wait for them. You might have an idea of what's going on, so you can twist it slightly and present it as your problem to them. Say you're having trouble with a co-worker who keeps taking credit for your work. You used to be friendly with them, but now you're so mad, you don't want to be around them. Unfortunately, you have to work together. You don't know what to do.

Your teen might perk up at this, especially if they are having problems with classmates or friends. Even if they are not, they might enjoy the chance to help you solve your problem. They might offer some good solutions, which can then open up a conversation. They saw that you were willing to get emotional with them, so they might feel safer, and more encouraged, to do the same.

These days, it can be tough to carve out time for your teen. Many parents are working from home and don't have an office space of their own where they can shut out the real world. Therefore, teens might come to you with a question or for help, and you'll feel like they are interrupting your work. It's also hard because everyone is connected constantly through their phones. If your teen sees you on your phone all of the time, even if it's for work or family matters, they'll emulate you. They'll turn to social media for friendship, attention, and validation. You'll learn more about that behavior in the next chapter, but for now, it's important to remember that your child sees you. Or, to be more specific, they might see the phone in front of your face. When you're stressed by work deadlines, it can be hard to put everything aside and listen to your teen. Even the most trivial information is still something they wanted to share with you, so you should value that.

If you feel like your teen is interrupting your work for attention, you can talk to them about set togetherness times. Maybe you sit down to dinner every night and talk about your days. Maybe you do something special with them once a week, so they get time with you alone. There are many ways to show your teen that they are still a priority without allowing your career to fall to the wayside. Scheduling time with your teen doesn't mean you see them just as something else to mark off your "to-do" list. In fact, it shows that you're prioritizing them by making a date you won't break.

Providing emotional support for your teen doesn't only mean that you let them come to you when needed or cry on your shoulder. You're also empowering them to make connections in the real world. Giving them a solid foundation of emotional support at home inspires them to go out and form relationships with others.

Your child has already encountered classmates and school friends for years. Maybe they have friends that live in the neighborhood or have joined clubs or teams. This is a great starting point to encourage relationships. You provide emotional support by asking your child about their friends and facilitating playdates.

Once you have a teenager, you can't even suggest something resembling a playdate, but you can make sure your teen knows that your house is always open. They are at that odd age where there isn't much to do. Hanging out at the library or community center might make them feel too young, but they can't get into a club or bar to hang out and talk. They might walk around at the mall or camp out at a table in the coffee shop, yet that can get old. If they know that they have the freedom to hang out at your house without you hovering over them or trying to make them play board games, they'll feel supported in that relationship.

If you don't encourage friendships or relationships, your teen might start to feel like you're suffocating them. You might ask them to come right home after school while they want to stay late with friends. They might lie to you and say they have a school club that afternoon just so they can culti-vate relationships. This lie might be the tip of the iceberg. If your teen feels like you're not encouraging their social life, they'll start keeping more from you.

This approach is especially detrimental when it's time for your teen to form romantic relationships. If you weren't accepting of friendships, they probably won't even attempt to tell you about a crush or first date.

On the other hand, if you've always encouraged an emotional connection with your child, they'll feel this as a teen. They'll have such a deep understanding of your love for them that they'll want to give it to others in turn. They'll become a great friend for everyone they encounter, and, in time, they will make a great, supportive partner because they had you as a role model.

This solid emotional support from you will also keep them on the right path when it comes to peer pressure. You'll learn more about this in Chapter 5, but it factors into emotional support and is worth briefly addressing here. If you've given your teen a happy home and plenty of emotional support, they'll feel connected to you. They've seen you model behavior for their whole lives, and they know what to do, or not do, when faced with peer pressure. Therefore, giving your teen emotional support helps them stay strong in a variety of relationships they'll experience throughout their lives.

IN SUMMARY

Knowing how to act in front of your teen is just as important as knowing how to interact with them.

- Many parents want to be friends with their kids or, alternately, rule very strictly in the hopes their kid never makes a bad decision. The real role of parenting is somewhere in the middle. It's a balancing act of being welcoming to your teen while also establishing rules, limits, and boundaries.

- Showing your teen how to act, from childhood and beyond, gives them an idea of what they can expect from the real world. They know how to act in society and make connections based on what you've taught them for their entire lives.
- Being a role model is a great way to teach your teen without them realizing you're teaching them. They watch you all of the time, so acting with intention, purpose, and empathy will pay off.
- Don't be afraid to show yourself as human. Adults aren't perfect, and if your teen knows that, they might feel more comfortable coming to you with their problems because they know you understand.
- Setting limits and boundaries can happen organically from the toddler years and up. If you didn't instill strong limits when your teen was younger, talk to them about it now. Let them know what you're comfortable with them doing, and outline any consequences they might face if they break the rules.
- There are steps that will help an emotional teen make logical decisions. Work through the decision-making steps with them by using a real or fictional example. Talking to them about how you'd work through it and sharing your experiences will help them see how they can do it in their own life.
- Above all, you want to be emotionally available for

your teen. It's hard when you have so much going on in your own life, but it creates a solid foundation of trust with your teen. They'll know that they can come to you about anything, and you'll put away your phone, work, or book and really listen to them.

- Providing emotional support for your teen benefits them in other relationships as well. They'll feel more secure in their relationships because you provide so much stability for them. They'll also have more empathy for those around them. This will help them feel more confident in who they are, which will protect against peer pressure and other issues that have become commonplace in their online environment.

3

THE ONLINE ENVIRONMENT OF THE NEW TEENS

Parents who have teens now have their own experience with the Internet. Most parents at least got online at school and probably researched most of their college coursework through the Internet. Many probably had the Internet at home and used it to keep online diaries, chat with friends, and more. Therefore, you understand the Internet and the appeal it has for teens, but you also understand how much it's changed in one generation.

The parents of teenagers probably used the Internet for a mix of fun and school. Your home computer might have been in the family room, and your parents walked by every so often to casually see what you were up to. Those days are gone. Teens have their own computers or laptops, not to mention tablets and phones. Parents of teens might not have gotten their own cell phone until they were in high school or college, and it only functioned as a phone. But teens these days get phones at younger and younger ages, and those devices are capable of everything.

SOCIAL MEDIA

Everyone has social media—even though most sites only allow people older than 13 to create an account. Preteens lie and make accounts when they are 11 or younger. Sometimes, their parents even make accounts for them with a promise to keep everything private to deter predators and unwanted attention.

Since teens have grown up with the Internet, sharing more of their lives online is no big deal. Everyone else does it, so it seems common and safe. They don't think anything of making a TikTok account because they already have Twitter, Facebook, and Instagram. It's just a new outlet to share content, so they sign up and open themselves up to countless benefits and harms.

Social media refers to any platform where people can upload and share content. Your teen might post text, photos, or videos. They can like and comment on others' information. Teens can share and click links, download materials, change other people's content and reupload, and more. Social media is constantly evolving, so it seems like anything is possible.

The Benefits of Social Media

Some adults want to completely villainize social media because of the few harms it creates and exacerbates, but it's not fair to address the harms without first going over the benefits. Like it or not, social media is here to stay. The platforms will evolve over time, but it will exist in some form or another for years to come.

The COVID-19 pandemic helped people of all ages realize how important the Internet is. So many companies were able to stay online and available to customers, clients, and employees due to this connectivity. This applied to teens as well. They were suddenly isolated from their friends, but with the Internet and social media, they could still connect.

Even when teens see their friends every day at school, there's still a security blanket in the form of social media. They know they are able to interact with their friends beyond school hours and often in different ways than they can at school.

Social media also lets teens connect to people they don't know. This can be a harmful side effect, yes, but as a benefit, you have to think about everything they get to learn. A teen in a small town can connect with teens who live in big cities and ride public transportation all over. They can get to know people in foreign countries, like a modern day pen pal connection.

If your teen is struggling with their identity, they can seek people online who have gone or are going through something similar. They can get tips, advice, help, and support from these individuals. While it's understandable that you'd prefer your teen come to you, it's not always their first choice. They might want to learn more about other identities before they come to you. They have a right to explore themselves before they bring you into the loop about their true self. The Internet and social media give them the opportunity to do this.

Social media also helps teens find outlets to express themselves. It's only normal that they don't want to tell you everything they do and think, but they don't want to keep it all inside, either. Essentially, posting online on a private account or messaging friends is a great way to get this out of their systems.

The popular platforms like Facebook, Twitter, Instagram, and TikTok aren't the only social media outlets your teen has access to. Many multiplayer games on Steam, PlayStation, and other consoles allow players to chat via text and voice. This counts as social media because your teen is meeting other people and interacting with them. They still need to have the same privacy standards as they do with things they post on other apps' news feeds.

Since the breadth of social media is so extensive, it's a great way for teens to explore their creativity. They are learning what content is posted online and will mimic what they see.

Teens will watch YouTube and then record their own videos. They can see an image, download it, change it, and make it their own. They can follow photographers and attempt to further their own camera skills.

When you talk with your teens about social media and your expectations for their online behavior, you're giving them permission to explore the Internet while also setting boundaries to keep them safe. They'll respect you being open with them and might even involve you in their online life.

Allowing your teen to safely use social media helps them develop digital media literacy. They'll understand how to behave online and what to keep private. They'll learn about settings that can reveal their location to others or share data from throughout their phone with one single app. This information will not only keep them safe now but help them with skills necessary for future jobs, schools, and more.

The Harms of Social Media

In a strange way, many of the benefits of social media can also be harmful. Sometimes, your teen doesn't need to be so connected to their friends and classmates. They might try to interact more with people through their devices and social media than be present with the family.

When people are linked through Twitter, Facebook, Instagram, TikTok, and more, then it's harder to separate relationships. Someone who is nice to your teen when they are playing World of Warcraft online might ignore them at school.; someone who acts nice to their face to keep from getting in trouble might bully them online or send inappropriate content.

These harms can happen whether your teen knows the perpetrator or not. They can get inappropriate spam emails. Someone on Facebook might find their Twitter and start harassing them across platforms. Some people are mean just to do it, and they don't care who their target is. They don't take it personally, but your teen probably will, and that can be detrimental to their emotional health and mental well-being.

Talking to your teen about social media means you have to talk about what it's appropriate for them to do, say, and post. You don't want your teen to be the one who's the bully. You don't want them to send an inappropriate picture to a crush and end up seeing it plastered across the Internet, and you want to make sure that they shouldn't do that with anyone else's picture, either.

If you're open in talking about the downsides of social media with your teen, they'll feel more comfortable coming to you with problems. When someone harasses them, makes them feel uncomfortable, or asks for personal information, they won't feel stuck and give in to the other person. They'll know they have your support and will come to you for advice and help.

In addition to establishing guidelines for social media use, you should also place time restrictions. It's too easy for your teen to spend time online—even if they are only spending 15 minutes on each app! And it's easy to lose track of time when you're hit with the rewards of scrolling and constantly seeing new content. Therefore, giving your teen a time limit and then putting their devices away will help them have a healthy relationship with social media.

Encourage them to talk to you about what they see and interact with. Ask them what they look for on social media and what they like about it. An open dialogue keeps you informed about what they are doing online as well as what's going on in their life. If there's an app you're unfamiliar with, ask your teen to tell you about it and show you how it works.

Some parents make their teens have private accounts, so strangers can't contact them as easily. You can also ask your teen to add you as a friend on any of their accounts, so you see what they are posting. Of course, doing this might mean they create a fake account for you and a different one where they post things you wouldn't approve of, but it might help to show them that you're interested in their online life. Instead of feeling like you're watching them and waiting for them to slip up, they might see it as you trying to get to know them in a deeper way.

It might feel tempting to outright ban social media until your teen hits a certain age, but this is rarely an effective tactic. Everyone is online, and your teen will find a way to access the apps. They'll feel like they have to hide it from you, which means they'll start lying to you about this side of their life and maybe other things, too. Since they already know you don't approve of social media, they might get reckless regarding what they post and endanger themselves physically, mentally, and emotionally.

Making social media taboo or not restricting your teen's access can lead to online addictions. They feel like they can't stop scrolling news feeds or else, they risk missing out on what others are doing. The sad reality is that they miss out on their own lives while they are looking at pictures and reading updates from others.

If your teen shares a lot online, the addiction is still there—just in a different form. They get dopamine hits when someone likes their pictures or updates. If someone comments, they either feel validation from a positive comment or crushing disappointment or anger from a negative comment. They start living for social media, thinking about what they can post to get likes and attention. They are not living their life for their own satisfaction and growth but rather for the approval of others.

Cyberbullying is a major downside of social media. It's worse than standard bullying because it has a large scope, and it can be hard to track down who is behind the accounts. Sometimes, your teen's classmates might make fake accounts to bully others, but it can also be random people around the world terrorizing people just because they can. Sometimes, there is no reason to why someone is a cyberbully or why they targeted your teen.

There are different types of cyberbullying. Intentional cyberbullying is when someone targets your teen specifically. They might make mean comments on things your teen posts. They might screenshot text and pictures and edit them to look and say different things that antagonize your teen. They might start rumors and spread them via social media.

Some cyberbullies don't care who they are hurting. They'll leave mean comments even though they don't know your teen. They might send inappropriate pictures or texts. They might even send threats, whether they know how to find your teen in real life or not.

It might be tempting to brush off cyberbullying because it only happens online, but you have to remember that your teen has an entire life online. Having their name or screen name muddied by cyberbullies can make it hard for them to feel safe online—even in communities where they initially felt welcomed. Since cyberbullies can stay relatively anonymous, your teen might not know who to trust and can have trouble finding the true identity of the bully.

Once something is on the Internet, it lives forever in one form or another. So, if a cyberbully is spreading rumors about your teen, that information will be accessible through search engines. People might screenshot the text or photos and share them as well. When a link or screenshot is shared, there's no way to control who might see it. The image lives on as a digital file forever.

It's equally likely that your teen is a victim of cyberbullying or acts as a cyberbully themselves. Since you don't have to show your face or use your real name online, it's easy to say anything you want. People feel empowered to say mean things because they don't have to face the consequences. However, there are real people behind the accounts, so it's important for your teen to know how to identify and avoid cyberbullying as well as not do it themselves.

THE STRATEGIES TO MINIMIZE SOCIAL MEDIA RISK

When you're balancing the benefits and harms of social media use, you need to be realistic. There's no way to protect your teen completely, so it's best to give them all the information possible and let them make informed decisions.

Know they can come to you with any problems. Many teens are cyberbullied and never tell anyone because they are embarrassed that a faceless screen name can torture them so badly, or they are ashamed of the information leaked or rumors started. By telling your teen about social media risks before anything happens, you're letting them know that you understand. You know what they might go through, so you're able to help them with it.

If your teen doesn't feel comfortable coming to you, you can try to pick up on clues that something is wrong. They might not talk to you as much as they used to. They might stop checking their phone or not want to get online much. They might seem like they have no energy or just want to stay locked in their room. They might act like they have no self-esteem. You'll learn in later chapters that these symptoms can signal depression and anxiety as well, so it doesn't mean your teen is having trouble on social media, but it's something to look out for.

The Strategies

Set up social media guidelines for both you and your teen to adhere to. Remember: You're their role model, and they'll follow your example. You can't be on your phone all of the time and expect them to put theirs away. Make time for them like you ask them to do for you. Having set times to check your social media and then putting devices away can hold the whole family accountable. Maybe it means you make time to have dinner together every night or have a weekly movie night. Taking breaks like this also helps everyone realize what's important—real life. Social media is fun and addicting, but you need to stay connected to reality and your loved ones.

You can also ask that your teen is only online friends with people they know in real life. If they have private social media accounts, they should only add people they know and trust. This keeps their photos and personal information relatively safe. People can still screenshot and share information, but at least you'd have an idea of who leaked the data.

Check the privacy levels of all of your teen's social media accounts. This isn't just ensuring they have a private account; it also relates to the data shared when they post an update. Many apps default to share locations since social media is meant to be instant. The apps share your location because you're most likely sharing a current photo to Instagram or tweeting about what you're doing at the moment. However, sharing this data is dangerous. Even on private accounts, your teen should never enable sharing their location.

Talk to your teen about what they are posting online. They shouldn't share personal information like their full name, date of birth, address, school, or current locations. They also shouldn't share risqué pictures. Make sure they understand that not all people are kind and might use their personal pictures with bad intentions. Talk to your teen about what these pictures look like and make sure you both feel comfortable with what they might post online. While having a private account and posting pictures of themselves is somewhat safer, there's still a risk of screenshots getting leaked, so they need to feel comfortable with anything they share online.

Let your teen know that they can block or report anyone who is harassing them online. Most apps make it easy to flag an account. If they can't figure out how to do it, help them take the right steps toward holding the cyberbully accountable.

If they are only friending people they know in real life, there's a slightly decreased risk of cyberbullying, but catfishing is big online. A catfish could steal the photos of one of your teen's friends and pose as them in an attempt to get access to their social media. Your teen can always verify identities by messaging friends or talking to them at school about what their screen names are, if they got hacked, and more. This open discourse increases the safety of their social circle online.

In case your teen is cyberbullied, provide a pillar of support for them. Encourage them to tell you everything or find a mental health professional they feel comfortable with. If the cyberbully is a classmate, it's possible to get teachers, principals, and guidance counselors involved.

IN SUMMARY

Social media has many pros and cons, so it's up to you and your teen to find the right outlets and guidelines for app usage.

- Social media can be beneficial for teens because it's an outlet for them. They can be themselves or stay anonymous while they explore their identity, interests, creativity, and hobbies.

- Social media allows teens to connect to people around the world. They can learn about different people and cultures in a way that previous generations couldn't.

- Being active on social media allows teens to stay in contact with their friends all the time. This gives them a source of support—even if they are physically alone. The true value of this connection was proven during the pandemic lockdown.

- Just because interaction can be a positive thing doesn't mean that social media has no downsides. There are many harms that might initially seem like benefits. Not being able to separate from classmates gives teens more platforms for bullying, abuse, and stalking. These platforms also have a wider breadth because they are public.

- Whether they are looking for it or not, teenagers can find a lot of inappropriate content online. It's easy to stumble across adult materials—even with parental controls in place. They can also be sent these materials directly from friends, enemies, or strangers.

- The popular social media apps are constantly changing, so it's harder for parents to stay up to date on them. They also all have unique privacy settings that can be tough to understand, so your teen might be broadcasting more personal data than they intend to.

- There's no way to completely avoid cyberbullying, but you can make the possible situation better by being proactive. Let your teen know that they can come to you with any online harassment or strange situations. Keep their accounts private and limited to people they actually know. Make sure they feel comfortable with the world, possibly seeing anything they post online. And, best of all, make sure their offline life is rich, so they are more inclined to put down their devices and have fun away from the Internet. This makes them less likely to get cyberbullies and also gives them more to look forward to offline.

4

THE TEENAGE EMOTIONAL
ROLLER COASTER

Experiencing anxiety and depression is a normal part of life; most people feel it several times a month, if not daily, in different situations. However, the way it presents in teens is more unique. Since they don't have the life experience of adults, even minor anxiety might seem like a big deal and send teens into a spiral. Most of their thinking is done in the emotional areas of the brain, so they can't stop and think rationally when faced with a situation that causes anxiety or depression.

Many things will cause teens stress that wouldn't phase them later in adulthood. Starting high school, finding their classes, opening their locker's combination lock, making new friends, and handling schoolwork are all sources of stress that adults don't have to deal with. They are also meant to be thinking about their future at this point, looking ahead to higher education and a career path.

Add into that mixture the new world of social media and your teen constantly being connected to others, either in positive ways or experiencing envy or cyberbullying, and the sources of stress are endless. When this stress is left unresolved, it can escalate into anxiety and depression.

ANXIETY

It's normal to feel anxious in various situations. This sensation is a natural reaction to being unsure of what's to come or not knowing how to act. For example, if your teen is going to make a speech in front of the whole school, they'll feel anxious. Not only is this expected but that feeling will actually help them deal with the nerves involved with the speech. They might feel like their heart is pounding, and their body is buzzing, which helps them push through the presentation.

Anxiety doesn't always give you a boost of adrenaline, though. Sometimes, especially for teens, anxiety can be crippling. If they are anxious about everyday situations, they'll start avoiding people and places, so they don't have to experience that feeling.

What Is Anxiety?

Anxiety is your brain telling you that a possible threat is near. It's meant to stir worry and awareness, so you know something is about to happen, and you're ready to protect yourself. It makes your brain and body feel on edge and ready for fight-or-flight mode. Your heart will pound, you might start breathing heavily, and your hands might shake. Temporary feelings like this are normal and even beneficial for your overall motivation, but your body can't function properly if this is a prolonged state.

Your teen most likely feels anxiety all of the time in the back of their mind. They are going through so many physical changes that they have to adjust to, so their body already feels strange to them. Then, they are experiencing so many new things in their physical life but also in their emotional life. There's always something for them to worry about, so they feel a constant buzz of anxiety. Some teens can push it to the back of their mind and work to make friends, join clubs, and get good grades until the anxiety fades when they get older. Yet many teens understandably can't juggle all of that at once. They live with a feeling of uneasiness, which can escalate into panic attacks and anxiety disorders.

Anxiety in Teens

While it's normal to feel anxiety, that feeling can escalate into an anxiety disorder. About 25% of teens have an anxiety disorder, and almost 6% have a severe anxiety disorder (Hurley, 2017). An anxiety disorder means the sensation of anxiety is severe enough to be detrimental to your teen's mental, emotional, and physical health. They might stop hanging out with friends, drop out of extracurricular sports and clubs, and avoid interacting with anyone. Their grades can plummet, and they are not interested in anything they used to enjoy.

Teen girls are more likely to experience panic disorder than boys, and it typically appears between the ages of 15 to 19 (Pruitt & American Academy of Child and Adolescent Psychiatry, 2000). They can either experience anxiety because of a specific cause or for no specific reason they can determine. This disorder is characterized by panic attacks, which happens when anxiety quickly ramps up to a degree your teen can't handle, resulting in physical and emotional distress. The panic attack begins in their mind but presents physically as a shortness of breath, pounding heart, sweating, dizziness, and nausea. Since all of the feelings hit your teen at once, they might think they are dying, which amplifies the negative feelings even more.

Once your teen experiences a panic attack, it's common for their general anxiety to increase. They know what a panic attack feels like and are worried about experiencing another one. As a result, they live in a constant state of anxiety, sure that the next panic attack is right around the corner.

Teens also experience phobias, which are exaggerated fears that feel too real to them but might not make sense to you. A phobia centers around a specific idea, object, or situation, and your teen is deathly afraid of it. The phobia is so prevalent that they'll do anything they can to avoid the possible situation, so they are not triggered. This is an exaggerated response because the source of a phobia isn't life-threatening. Your teen's anxiety just causes them to blow up the fear until it feels like it actually poses a threat to them.

Identifying the Signs of Anxiety

It's hard to see the signs of anxiety sometimes because teens are already going through so many changes. If your teen is avoiding you, it might seem like business as usual, especially if they've been moody lately, and you've argued. Since teens are on an emotional roller coaster, you might think they seem anxious one day and then back to normal the next, but there are patterns you can look for to identify the signs of anxiety.

Teens react differently to anxiety. You know your child best, so you'll probably be able to pick up on their anxiety based on the following signs.

Some teens keep their anxiety pushed deep down inside of them. They are constantly worried or afraid of any range of things in their lives, which can show as a tendency to be overly cautious. They might not speak until they are certain no one else is going to speak, and everyone else is listening. They might constantly look around to see who's nearby. They might constantly check their planner to ensure they've completed every homework assignment and studied for all upcoming tests.

This hypervigilance can also present as restlessness. If your teen seems like they can't sit still, it might be because they have too much on their mind. When worries are making them feel anxious, they can't physically sit still because their brain is in overdrive. Getting up and wandering around might help them feel like they are not just stewing in their own fears.

Social anxiety can appear when teens are among friends, family, or strangers. They won't interact with others much, appearing uncomfortable in the company. If someone asks them a question, they might only answer with one word. On the other hand, they could get overly emotional when talking to someone else as if they turned on a faucet of emotions and can't turn it off. Both situations will further exacerbate their anxiety because they know it's not the way to act around others, yet they can't help themselves.

Anxiety can also present in physical symptoms. Anxiety is a form of stress and worry, so many people suffering from it keep their body tense. Your teen might have tight shoulder or back muscles. They might clench their jaws and experience headaches. Anxiety can also lead to stomach cramps and nausea because they are so preoccupied with the worry that they are making themselves physically ill. Since anxiety relates to nervousness, they might also flush, sweat, tremble, and fidget.

Teens experiencing severe anxiety might change their habits suddenly. Maybe they used to be ravenous after school and eat a snack while the family gathered in the kitchen, but now, they say they aren't hungry and go hide in their room. They might also not eat when the family goes out for dinner together or not use public restrooms. This could be because they are hyperaware of themselves and others and feel too anxious and self-conscious to do anything in public they think will call attention to themselves.

They can also have trouble falling asleep and staying asleep. The anxiety is in their brain nonstop, so they genuinely can't stop their mind from thinking long enough to get rest. This lack of rest can result in other physical signs, like circles under their eyes, constant yawning, losing weight, and more.

Emotional signs include being emotional often, whether they are crying, yelling, or giving you the silent treatment. They might strive for perfectionism and worry about making a mistake—even if it's minor. You constantly reassure them that there aren't major consequences resulting from the error.

On the other hand, they might close themselves off from you and not take any feedback or criticism—even if you deliver it gently. They might seem standoffish or aloof, but they are really trying to protect themselves from that feeling of failing to meet your expectations.

Obsessive thoughts are key to anxiety. Teens will constantly think about their schoolwork, friend group, or the future. Even if things are out of their control, they won't stop worrying about it. This could even lead to nightmares where they experience everything that happens in their imagination, which again circles back to a lack of sleep.

All of these actions tie together to present as behavioral changes in your teen. They might close themselves off from any social situation, whether it's with family, friends, sports teams, or other extracurricular clubs. They might refuse to talk or interact with others, and some teens even let it go so far that they can't go to school. Their anxiety is so severe that they can't handle going to the building and going through the motions of participating in classes and interacting with classmates and teachers.

Some teens dread school because it separates them from their loved ones. Anxiety can present as attachment, so your teen might become glued to your side instead of closing you out completely. As much as you might like the attention and affection they are giving you, if it's drastically different from how they usually act, it's a sign of ongoing anxiety and should be addressed as such.

DEPRESSION

Teenagers are on an emotional roller coaster, so along with the extreme highs are the deep lows. They might even tell you that they feel "down in the dumps," but most likely, you can pick up on their cues when they aren't feeling at the top of their game.

Teens are changing so much in adolescence, so it's no surprise they experience depression, whether it's brief or lingering. Their bodies and minds are changing drastically. They are tackling new schools, like middle school, high school, and college. They feel pressure to do well, so they don't ruin their future. And adults are asking them what they want to be when they grow up—even though they might not have a clue yet.

All of these changes and questions feel like pressure to teens, and this pressure gets heavier until they feel like they can't handle anymore. Sometimes, it starts as stress or confusion, but once it starts to feel like too much, it's depression.

Teens aren't only experiencing their own highs and lows. They are old enough to follow the news and can get a lot of current event information from social media. They are constantly seeing the stories that make the world look hopeless, so they are aware of the threats out there in the world. Even if your teen is making good choices and staying safe, they are learning about mass shootings, bombings, diseases, and more. With the harsh realities of the world right always on their minds, it's no surprise that teens experience depression.

What Is Depression?

Depression is a medical condition that impacts your mind, emotions, and behavior. It seems insurmountable, but it's treatable with therapy and medication, if needed. When you experience depression, you get no enjoyment from life. All of the hobbies that used to give you purpose feel empty. You don't see the point of completing tasks to get you through the day because you're overcome with hopelessness. With the weight of this emotional state, your physical health can deteriorate since you're not taking care of yourself. You'll notice that you're backsliding into a state where you don't care about anything.

There are degrees of depression ranging from mild to severe. Regardless of the severity, you most likely feel some level of symptoms like sadness, loss of interest in anything, lack of appetite, overeating just to do something, not sleeping, sleeping all the time, lack of energy, and feeling worthless. People suffering from depression might have trouble focusing on anything or making decisions.

When depression is very severe, thoughts of suicide can escalate. Many mildly depressed people think of death, but it's usually more abstract. Severe depressives might plan out their own death, whether they have the energy to follow through or not.

To be classified as depression, these symptoms need to last more than two weeks. Anything less is seen as a temporary sadness. If your depressive state is drastically different from your typical levels of function, then you'll most likely be diagnosed with major depressive disorder.

Depression in Teens

Symptoms of depression for teens might look different than it does for adults. The general premise is the same: Your teen feels sad and hopeless, so their desire to do anything fades. Activities that used to make them feel proud or bring them joy don't matter anymore. They think, act, and feel differently than they used to. Depression can even present as physical problems and ailments, along with impacting your teen mentally and emotionally.

Teens are on a roller coaster of emotions every single day, so it's no surprise that they might feel sad after experiencing peer pressure, a loss of a friendship, a bad grade, or their changing body. However, if they stay in that low mood for an extended period, then it's not just a lull in the roller coaster: It's depression.

Depression is a serious mental state that shouldn't be brushed off as a phase. Telling your teen to look at the bright side will only make them feel worse. They'll wonder why they can't shake the sadness instead of realizing that it's a serious disorder which mental professionals can help them tackle. Acknowledging depression as a real condition will help your teen understand they can come to you with their problems and know that you'll support them.

Teens will show depression by being irritable with everyone they encounter. They are sensitive to criticism, which might seem related to the irritability and perhaps only focused on the adults in their lives, but you'll notice it has a broader scope than the stereotypical moody teenager.

Depression in teens can also display as aches and pains. Again, it's hard to discern these from standard growing pains since their bodies are changing so much, but these issues won't be linked to any physical changes they are going through and might last longer, like depression does.

Identifying the Signs of Depression

Knowing the signs of depression can help you support your teen when they are navigating this issue. There are emotional and behavioral symptoms you can watch for, so you know when to step in and help your teen during these troubling times.

Emotional changes include your teen feeling sad all of the time and crying for no reason. They might lock themselves away from others, whether they are afraid of showing emotions or just can't be around anyone else. They think no one understands what they are feeling, so they don't even want to try to relate to others.

They don't react well to criticism or feedback—even if it's well-intended on your behalf. They feel like no one understands them, and everyone is picking on them, but nothing matters anyway. This makes them extremely sensitive, so you might find yourself constantly reassuring them that they are worthy of love, attention, and good things.

Depressed teens feel hopeless and deflated. They don't look forward to their future—no matter what they have planned for high school, college, and beyond. They feel empty and don't care about it anymore. In addition to not caring about the future, they don't care about now. They don't enjoy the hobbies, sports, or extracurriculars they used to love. They might feel less self-esteem, whether it's the effect of not partaking in their usual hobbies or the cause. They feel worthless in their life and don't know what role they are playing in the world. They might even feel guilty that they are alive when others aren't. This guilt can also mean they bring up things from the past that embarrassed them or previous examples of failure. Everything looks bleak to a teen with depression.

Some teens can keep the emotional signs of depression hidden; you'll be able to pick up on their behavioral changes. Depressed teens always look and act tired because their sleeping patterns are disrupted. They are either unable to sleep at all or want to sleep all of the time, but either way, their bodies are lagging.

Though they appear tired, some depressed teens might also be restless and twitchy. They might pace because they can't be still. They'll sit down and promptly get right back up. They always seem physically agitated, and some part of their body is always moving.

Many teens have changes in appetite when they are depressed. They eat all of the time because they want to feel some joy from junk food or feeling full, but they are not hungry when they eat. On the other hand, they might stop eating because they don't see a point in trying to nourish their body.

When your teen is depressed, they don't care about their schoolwork—even if they were once a top student. Their grades will suffer, and they won't participate in class like they used to. They might even skip school or tell you they are sick just so they can stay home.

Some teens engage in risky behavior like self-harm or drug and alcohol abuse when they are depressed. They are so desperate to feel something that they go to extremes. These behaviors are so important that you'll learn more about them in the next chapter.

IN SUMMARY

Teens are experiencing so many changes as their bodies and brains mature. It's only natural that they'll feel anxious and depressed, but if you notice the signs, you can help them get through these rough patches.

- Anxiety is a common feeling that makes you feel on edge when you're nervous or worried. It can be uncomfortable, but it often motivates people to do things they are afraid of. Prolonged feelings of anxiety, however, are detrimental to your teen's mental, physical, and emotional health.

- It can be tough to see the signs of anxiety because they present differently in every person. Teens are already on an emotional roller coaster, so you might not notice that they are suffering from this sensation. Staying aware of what they are going through in their daily lives will help you notice anxiety.

- Teens don't experience depression just because of things going on in their own lives. They are aware of the world at large and current events, and they feel pressure and sadness because of the hopelessness these issues convey. They are taking the weight of the world on their shoulders because they know their generation is going to have to change the future.

- Depression appears differently in teens than it does in adults. Knowing what to look for in terms of their behavior, emotional expressions, and outward appearance will help you know when your teen needs the most support.

- Teens can feel sad for days at a time without being depressed; it's just part of their journey. However, if their behavior greatly changes and stays detrimental for two weeks or more, they are most likely depressed.

5

WHAT CAN IT LEAD TO?

Learning about the detrimental sides of anxiety and depression has given you an idea of what teens are feeling. They have the weight of the world on their shoulders, but they are too young and inexperienced to handle that. Since they are feeling either too much or nothing, it's not surprising that they'd turn to destructive behavior. Some teens are trying to numb their anxiety, while others are so depressed that they are just trying to feel *something*.

Suicide rates have been steadily rising among teenagers since 2007—all in data compiled even before the pandemic (Dastagir, 2020). This time period coincides with the prevalence of social media, but you can't just blame that one outlet. With the physical changes and emotional turmoil preteens and teens are experiencing from the ages of 10 to 24, it's not surprising that they are looking for some form of escape.

Also, their logical minds aren't fully developed at those ages, so they most likely don't realize the wide reach their suicide would have on their family, friends, and even classmates. They are suffering and just want that feeling to stop, so they take rash actions.

Being aware of what your teen is feeling when they experience anxiety and depression will help you relate to them in deeper ways. It will also ensure you see the warning signs when their physical, mental, and emotional health is getting worse. It's just as important to know what these feelings can lead to, whether it's substance abuse, self-harm, or suicide.

SUBSTANCE ABUSE: ALCOHOL AND DRUGS

Many teens explore substances because they are curious, and their friends might be trying them as well. Depending on your rules with your teen, some exploration is normal and even encouraged in safe measures. However, using substances to escape normal life and problems is a slippery slope, and your teen should never have a dependency on substances to get through the day. Both alcohol and drugs are detrimental for the teenage brain and body, so make sure you're aware of what your teen is doing.

Alcohol

Research has found that 29% of teens drink alcohol and 14%binge drink. About 17% of teens have ridden in a car driven by an intoxicated driver, and 5% have driven drunk themselves (Pedrelli et al., 2016). Alcohol is one of the easiest substances for teens to acquire. They can have older friends buy it for them or use their own fake IDs. Some places don't even check ID if the person looks old enough, so it's easy for younger teens to get beer if they are tall or developed early. They might also find it in their parents' liquor cabinets or the refrigerator.

Alcohol is a socially acceptable substance as well. Many adults drink socially, go to bars for fun, or get buzzed or drunk, and teens notice this. If it's okay for adults, they think it's safe for them as well—even though their bodies and brains aren't fully developed yet.

Most teens are going to try beer or a mixed drink at a party during their high school years, and this isn't cause for alarm. However, if your teen seems to rely on alcohol as a crutch, is getting buzzed or drunk often, and lets alcohol interfere with their daily life, then they have a problem. This is a sign that they have a deeper problem, like anxiety or depression, and are trying to medicate themselves with alcohol and possibly other substances.

Teens who don't want to talk about their anxiety and depression, or perhaps don't know what they are experiencing, are drawn to alcohol because it's easy to obtain. They can have beers or drinks at a party, and their friends and classmates will just think they are cutting loose and having fun. They are getting buzzed or drunk along with everyone else—even though your teen is actually drinking because they are trying to make themselves feel better. It can also help them feel more social if they are usually awkward around groups of people.

Many teens will drink whenever they can in order to get out of their head and not feel as bad as they normally do when they are overcome with anxiety and depression. It's easier, in many cases, to drink alcohol instead of pinpointing the problem, talking to parents, seeing a doctor, and getting the proper prescription to make them feel better.

However, alcohol doesn't make them feel better for long. They start needing more and more to get a buzz. The hangover the next day makes everything seem worse, and alcohol can disrupt sleep as well. An anxious teen who already has trouble sleeping might get temporary relief from their thoughts when they are drunk, but the next day, they'll feel more tired, grumpier, and more anxious than before. Alcohol seems like a coping mechanism at the moment, but it makes things worse when it wears off.

Being buzzed or drunk further impairs the teenage mind. They already made impulsive decisions because their logical brain isn't developed, but alcohol makes it worse. They make irrational decisions and partake in risky behaviors, including driving drunk or riding with a drunk driver, stealing, skipping school, vandalizing property, and hurting themselves.

They might also become sexually promiscuous because alcohol lowers their inhibitions. When teens are drunk, they are more likely to be coerced into sex—even if they don't want it or instigate it themselves. Whether it's consensual or not, many of these drunk sexual encounters don't involve protection, which puts your teen at more of a risk, physically.

If teens start drinking at a young age, the alcohol can impair their growth. Heavy alcohol use slows bone growth and can delay puberty. It also affects their brain and can cause their grades to plummet. Teens who drink often will have trouble remembering things and might even start to lose verbal skills and visual-spatial cognition. As their mind loses capacity to learn and retain information, they might prefer to skip school or drop out completely.

Symptoms of Alcohol Abuse

Half of all teens who have a mental health disorder will also have a substance abuse problem unless their mental health is prioritized and treated (Pedrelli et al., 2016). This risk increases due to genetics. If you have an alcohol problem or have a family history of addictions, then your teen most likely has the same issue. Females are also more at risk for having concurrent disorders, such as mental health and addictions. It's also likely that people experiencing a depressive or anxious episode will try to calm themselves with alcohol, so in some cases, it can be hard to pinpoint which condition leads to which problem.

When you start noticing signs of anxiety and depression in your teen, try to find out if they've been drinking as well. Sometimes, drinking heavily or binge drinking at parties can cause depressive episodes, which your teen then tries to alleviate with more drinking; the cycle then worsens and continues.

The symptoms of a buzzed or drunk teen are the same as those of an adult, including alcohol on their breath, slurred speech, and trouble walking. They might not be able to reach out and grab something without missing it or have other coordination problems. They might fall down or bump into things as they are walking through the house.

However, you won't always see your teen when they are drunk. They might drink at sleepovers or while they are out and then be relatively sober by the time they get home. In that case, you'll want to look for more underlying symptoms of alcohol abuse.

You can also check and see if your teen seems more tired than usual or talks about aches and pains that don't seem to have a source or cause. They might try to hide things from you more than before and act guilty for what they are doing. Instead of coming clean, they might be really nice and helpful for a period before they drink again and continue that cycle as well. Anxiety, irritation, and sadness are also behaviors you'll see with alcohol abuse. They might stop participating in hobbies they used to enjoy.

You'll notice that many of these symptoms are the same as what you'd see for anxiety and depression as well. That makes it really hard to find out the root cause of your teen's issues. Always having an open line of communication can help you help them. If you ask them if they are feeling anxious or depressed, they might answer if they know they are going to get support from you instead of judgment. However, if they are abusing alcohol, they might not answer you because they are trying to hide their real problem.

Research has found that teens who abuse alcohol don't get help or find treatment (National Institute on Alcohol Abuse and Alcoholism, 2019). They are more likely to go to their doctor for treatment for a problem that's caused by, or related to, alcohol consumption than for the alcohol problem itself. Therefore, it's incredibly important that you, as a parent, watch for the signs of alcohol abuse, so you can help your teen.

An untreated mental disorder as a teen can also lead to substance abuse later in adulthood. If you think your teen is suffering from anxiety or depression, it's best to seek professional help before things get out of hand.

Treatment for Alcohol Abuse

Treating mental disorders as well as alcohol abuse will involve a different approach than just treating addiction. It's always best to involve a professional, and they can help you and your teen find the right path. In some cases, they might choose to treat the addiction first and then the mental disorder. Sometimes, they will try to treat both conditions at the same time to improve your teen's overall health instead of hoping to see improvement in one area before moving on to the next.

Traditional 12-step programs aren't as effective for teens because they feel stressed out by the rules and meetings, so it's better to find a professional they trust and try one-on-one or small group therapy. This intimate environment will help them feel more supported and less embarrassed by what they might think of as a flaw or mistake. Providing a stress-free treatment option for them will not only help them realize their problem can be overcome but also help them feel empowered to do it themselves. If they feel capable of that, it can help them see that they are responsible for their lives and behavior, so they are more likely to make good choices in the future.

When teens take recovery into their own hands, they'll have help from the professional through cognitive behavioral therapy (CBT). This therapy helps them manage alcohol withdrawal and depressive symptoms at the same time. Adding in the social support of small group therapy helps teens see that they are not alone in what they are going through. They'll feel supported by the others in the group and also empowered that they are in a position to help others as well. Having a social circle going through recovery with them can help them see what they have to offer other people as well. Once they are confident in who they are in this small group therapy, they'll feel stronger in themselves in other social situations and will be less likely to turn back to alcohol as a coping mechanism.

Drugs

It's fairly easy for most teens to get their hands on alcohol, but drugs can be a different matter. Some teens might not have access to street or illegal drugs but can abuse prescription drugs—either their own or those prescribed to others.

Teens take drugs for reasons similar to why they drink alcohol, but in this case, it's usually more for themselves. Taking drugs at parties is a way to be seen, but in many cases, it's a less visual addiction than drinking can be. Drinking is socially acceptable, so teens stand around with beers or red cups of mixed drinks. However, taking drugs is stereotypically a more covert action. Still, if your teen's friends are talking about taking drugs, your teen might feel peer pressure to do so—even if they don't do it together.

There are so many changes and sources of stress during puberty and the years of adolescence, and some teens try to cope with all of this by escaping into drugs. The pressure of making good grades, keeping friends, being nice to family members, and planning for their future is too much, and teens just want something to make them forget all of their problems. This is just in standard cases as well; if a teen is already suffering from anxiety or depression, then these stressors seem even heavier to them.

Studies have found that most teenagers try drugs because of peer pressure (Substance Abuse and Mental Health Services Administration, 2014). A friend, someone in their social circle, or someone at a party has drugs on hand and offers to share them, so teenagers feel inclined to partake. They want to fit in and be accepted by their peers. This is especially true in the cases of teens suffering from mental disorders because they want to seem normal and think that doing things other kids are doing will help them feel that way all of the time.

Other teens will start to use drugs to medicate themselves or escape their mental troubles. They are so sick of being stuck in their own mind, whether they are suffering from depression or anxiety, that they just want to feel something different—or nothing at all. Some drugs are uppers and will make them feel happy, productive, and manic. Others are downers and will put them to sleep or just make them mellow out and forget their problems.

Some teens try drugs just to experiment like they might with alcohol. They want to try something or seem more grown up, and they have access to the drug or alcohol, so they experiment. This can be harmful if they hurt themselves or others or try to drive when they are impaired. But, in a safe environment, experimenting can be acceptable for some teens.

Teens with anxiety and depression rarely just experiment, though. It might start out that way, but when they realize how the drugs make them feel, they might want that feeling more and more. This is how their addiction and dependence begins.

Symptoms of Drug Abuse

Noticing the signs of drug abuse can be hard depending on what your teen is taking. They might take an upper to get through the school day and seem fine by the time they come home; also, their personality might be changing so much due to their hormones and life stresses that you can't be sure if they are just irritable with you because they are a teenager or because they are on something. Teens try out different personalities as they try to discover who they really are, so it's tough to tell sometimes.

Many parents fear asking their kid if they are on drugs, only to offend their teen and have a door slammed shut in their face—both literally and figuratively. Accusing a teen of drug abuse and being wrong can damage your relationship and possibly sever methods of communication, so it can feel risky to approach your child about this.

A lot of the symptoms of drug abuse are the same as with anxiety, depression, and alcohol abuse, so involving a professional if you notice these signs is always a practical idea. Alcohol usually mellows people out, but drugs can either mellow them or make them energetic, so it can be harder to pinpoint the cause.

Strange sleeping patterns or lack of sleep can be a sign of drug problems. If your teen's weight rapidly changes and they stop eating, this is another symptom. They might have little to no energy or, conversely, too much energy, and come across as manic. This lack of energy or manic mindset can impact their school performance. They might act irritable when they are around the house. Some teens with drug problems fantasize about suicide, talk about it, or perhaps even gather the necessary supplies.

Your teen might start skipping school or letting their grades suffer. They might stop attending clubs, sporting events, and other extracurriculars they used to care greatly about. They act irritably or show otherwise drastic changes in their personality and behavior. They stop spending time with family or even try to avoid being together.

If your teen is using drugs and then stops for a while, you might notice signs of withdrawal. They might look sick or even get physically ill. Their limbs might shake, and they can't keep down any food.

Drug use goes hand in hand with mental disorders, so if you notice the symptoms of one, it might be a sign that your teen is dealing with both. If your teen is on prescription drugs for a medical or mental condition, make sure they are not abusing that prescription first of all. Changes in medication doses can impact their behavior in a way similar to street drugs or prescriptions they are not acclimated to. Their body is used to handling a certain amount of a pill, so if they are taking more, their body can't handle it, and you'll be able to tell the difference.

Treatment for Drug Abuse

Most treatment for drug abuse tackles the mental issue and the drug problem at the same time. Professionals know the importance of improving both factors or else, there's a higher chance of a relapse. Poor mental health will make your teen crave the drugs that help them escape. Similarly, their body will still crave the drugs—even if they are mentally in a better place. Therefore, treating both at once will keep your teen mentally and physically healthy and empowered to resist their former addictions.

Professionals will recommend therapy for mental issues, so your teen can talk through their troubles. Some professionals will have individual sessions for privacy but later suggest group therapy. The group setting helps your teen socialize in a safe environment. They feel supported by other teens that have also struggled and know what they are going through. They'll also feel more comfortable going back to school and friendships if they've had some time to interact with others with no drugs involved.

In the case of drug abuse, it's also important for teens to detox. This can be harmful if they try to do it on their own or even if you try to help them. Medical professionals can help them come off of their addictions without further harming their physical and mental health.

Teens with severe addictions might benefit from residential programs. It can feel hard to send your teen away because you'll miss them and also feel sad that you couldn't help them on your own, but sometimes, it's the best thing for them. They'll get full support in a short-term or long-term program and can reacclimate to life with no drugs involved. There are also outpatient treatments available.

Some professionals will also encourage family therapy. Your teen might have been the person with the addiction, but it affected everyone. Talking together with a certified therapist can help the whole family understand what happened and why. Together, you can all make a plan to move forward in a way that's healthy for everyone. Therapists will also help you figure out how to prevent relapses from happening.

SELF-HARM

Self-harm occurs when teens hurt themselves on purpose to try and feel something. They are not trying to die by suicide, but the behaviors they are exhibiting do hurt them physically. Blood might be involved, such as with cutting, or they are just trying to feel in control of something in their lives, like their body with eating disorders.

Cutting and eating disorders aren't the only types of self-harm, but they are among the most frequently occurring, so you'll learn the most about them. Other self-harm behaviors include burning or branding their skin, strangling themselves, overdosing on their prescriptions, banging their head on things, holding their breath until they feel dizzy or pass out, or other harmful behaviors that can hurt them physically and mentally.

These behaviors occur frequently, so watch for patterns. If your teen holds their breath and gets dizzy once that you notice, it might not be a form of self-harm, but you should keep an eye on their behavior. It can escalate, as they realize it makes them feel good or more in control of their life.

Many adults and even medical professions don't understand why teens hurt themselves. Most people don't like to feel pain, so to inflict it on yourself feels foreign. However, teens often want to be in control of some aspect of their life. They are at an age where they have to answer to teachers, parents, and possibly bosses. They have to eat breakfast, lunch, and dinner at set times. They have to complete homework and turn it in. They don't have much impact on their own life or freedom, so harming themselves is something they can do alone. They hold the razor blade and decide when and where to cut themselves. They feel power because they can inflict pain like that on themselves when no one else can.

Teens suffering from anxiety and depression especially appreciate this small measure of control they have over their lives and bodies. When they can't control their thoughts, worries, fears, and sadness, they at least feel glad that they have this power.

Self-harm can be influenced by peer pressure, like alcohol and drug abuse. Teens who participate in self-harm might have friends who do it also, or they might keep it to themselves. Sometimes, showing off cuts and scars is a source of pride for teens, but sometimes, they feel ashamed of it. Some teens harm themselves because they have low self-esteem. They might experience abuse or bullying and want to hurt themselves more than anyone else can. Some teens who harm themselves think of suicide, and cutting and harming themselves can be a way to test the waters and see what they are capable of.

Cutting

People who don't understand cutting often think it's just teens seeking attention. They want to bleed and show scabs and scars, so you know how much they are hurting. However, this isn't true, and many teens wear long sleeves to cover any cuts they might make on their arms. They are not trying to make you look at them; they are just trying to relieve their tension, stress, sadness, or anger. Sometimes, the feeling of pain helps them disconnect from their daily life and distracts them from other problems they are experiencing.

Just like with drug and alcohol abuse, cutting only gives minor relief from your teen's stress. It actually leads to more problems, like them stopping the blood flow and safely bandaging their wounds, so they'll heal without infection.

Cutting is most common in young teen girls, but that doesn't mean they are the only ones who participate in this behavior. Up to 30% of teens admit to harming themselves at some point (Iannelli, 2010). There's no set type of teen who cuts themselves; it can be depressed teens, impulsive teens, or even overachievers.

Symptoms of Cutting

Cutting is a physical form of self-harm, so it's easiest to notice symptoms by checking your teen. However, they are teenagers and have their own autonomy, so asking them to show you their skin isn't always going to fly with them. They are private and possibly feel strange about what their body is going through, so asking them to show you their arms or legs isn't the way to get them to open up to you.

You can see signs of cutting by watching what your teen wears. Maybe they are wearing long sleeves more often or when the weather doesn't call for it. They might wear pants when shorts would be the more weather-appropriate choice. Typically, the arms, wrists, and thighs are the most common locations for cutting. These areas are easy to keep hidden, but if your teen is covering these areas in hot weather or at the pool or beach, it might be a sign of something else.

It's important to not accuse them of cutting—even if they are wearing a sweatshirt at the beach. Many teens, especially girls, are uncomfortable with their changing bodies. It's better to have a kind discussion with them about why they feel the need to cover their body. You might find that they've been teased or even sexually harassed at school or elsewhere for showing their body, so they prefer to hide away. Girls who have been raped or molested also often cover themselves with out-of-season clothes, so being diplomatic in your approach is crucial.

Not all teens hide proof of their cutting. They might have cuts or burns on their hands, arms, legs, belly, or neck. They either can't cover some of these areas or don't want to, so if you see any cuts, scabs, or scars that don't look like accidents or appear very frequently, make note of it, so you can talk to your teen.

Emotional problems like anxiety, depression, and extreme outbursts of either anger or sadness can also reveal that your teen is harming themselves. Of course, the standard behaviors relating to anxiety and depression also apply here. Since these emotional issues are the undercurrent of many behaviors like drug and alcohol abuse or self-harm, it's important to watch for those symptoms as well.

If you think you see signs of cutting, don't confront your teen from a place of anger. It's always best to come to them gently, with kindness, in a place where they feel comfortable. Ask them if they are hurting themselves first, and don't just start with an accusation. If they say no, you can tell them what you noticed that made you think they were. If they say yes, comfort them and don't get angry at their behavior. Don't scold them or overreact to their harm. Tell them that you want to help. Cutting is usually a sign of a bigger issue, so you can start asking them about depression, anxiety, and other issues you think they might be experiencing. Let them know you're here to support them and can help them find the right professional that will support them while they work to feel better.

Treatment for Cutting

It's important to get professional treatment if your teen is cutting themselves. This is a dangerous form of self-harm because they are opening their skin, losing blood, and potentially inviting infections into their bodies. If they cut the wrong spot or too deeply, they might not be able to stop the bleeding. If they don't properly clean the cut, it might get infected, which can lead to very severe health issues. If they don't bandage it right, it might not heal or will leave a thick scar.

When teens don't get treatment for cutting, they can have problems later in life because they haven't learned how to properly cope with life. They might keep cutting themselves deeper or in different places to get the same release they did as teens. Their harm might escalate into more severe forms. They also might not be able to form serious relationships or friendships; have intimacy with another person; or feel pride in themselves and who they are. Cutting can be not only a release for them but also a shame that marks them as "other" and keeps them from relating to people around them.

Contacting a professional will help you find the right path of treatment for your teen if they are cutting. You might find that psychotherapy will help because your teen will have the space to talk to someone who understands them and can support them. You can always ask your teen what they are thinking and feeling, but they might not tell you the full story. Your teen will feel more comfortable opening up to a psychotherapist because they might be too ashamed to tell you everything they are going through. They'll be able to share all of the problems that are bothering them and leading them to cut. The psychotherapist can then help them sort out their troubles and emotions and move forward with a healthy way of life.

Psychiatry is another option of treatment for cutting. Usually, you have to go through your teen's medical doctor or a psychotherapist to get referred to a psychiatrist, but sometimes, you can make an appointment directly. These professionals will evaluate your teen and then prescribe medication to help them get past their troubles. If your teen also has depression, finding a psychiatrist is a great option because they can also prescribe antidepressants. Medication isn't meant to be a bandage for your teen's problems, but rather a way to balance their brain chemicals and help them think logically and feel in control.

There are also treatment centers for self-harm. They might call it self-injury or self-mutilation as well. These centers are inpatient or outpatient and specialize in helping people who hurt themselves. The professionals there will most likely use a mix of individual and group therapy to get to the root of your teen's problems. From there, they'll work to help your teen find healthier ways to deal with their pain and anger.

Support groups are also effective forms of treatment, especially if they are used in conjunction with psychotherapy or psychiatry. Your teen will have a chance to meet other people who also struggle with mental pain and harm themselves. They'll learn about how other people overcome this compulsion and stop cutting themselves. They'll also have a support system that they can lean on when they feel like they are struggling or backsliding and need some words of encouragement.

Eating Disorders

Eating disorders are very common in teens. Every 10 out of 100 girls will suffer from an eating disorder when they are going through adolescence (American Academy of Child and Adolescent Psychiatry, 2019). Some of it is because American society places so much importance on women's looks, especially their weight. Girls experience disordered eating and diets from young ages because they feel societal pressure to stay thin and be deemed attractive. However, that isn't the only reason that people have eating disorders, and females aren't the only ones who experience them.

98 | S.L. CLARK

Males can suffer from eating disorders, too. They might want to be tall and lanky or bulk up with muscle. They might be overweight, and other boys in school tease them. As a result, boys starve themselves or only eat certain foods. They may consume a lot of energy drinks or protein powder and try to get the stereotypical masculine look.

Anorexia and bulimia are the most common eating disorders. Anorexia is when a teen refuses to eat food. They see themselves as fat, no matter how skinny they may actually be. They literally starve themselves to lose weight. Since their body isn't getting the necessary nutrients, this is a very dangerous way to live. It can lead to dehydration, hormonal problems, and damage to internal organs. In extreme cases, it can even lead to death.

Bulimia is when teens eat a whole bunch of food, often junk food or unhealthy choices, and then purge the food from their body. They might make themselves throw up or take laxatives to get the food out. If their bodies absorb the food before they can get rid of it, they might exercise exhaustively to work off the calories they consumed. Since a bulimic teen is eating high-calorie foods and then throwing them up, their body isn't getting the nutrients and vitamins it needs. Constantly throwing up or using laxatives also causes harm to internal organs and body systems, like the throat and intestines.

Binge eating can occur without throwing up. If your teen is eating too much and not stopping when they are full, or making poor food choices, they could still benefit from professional help.

Extreme dieting also counts as an eating disorder. There doesn't have to be binging and purging or starvation involved for your teen to be endangering their health. It's best to make sure they are eating healthy foods, taking vitamins, and getting all of the nutrients they need, so they can grow strong.

Eating disorders are connected with depression because of the general sense of unhappiness your teen feels. They aren't happy with their life, their looks, or anything they are experiencing, so they try to control it in any way they can. That might mean they binge and purge, or maybe they starve themselves. Maybe they overeat or don't eat enough. They are just trying to make their body look and feel a certain way, and food is their way to control that when everything else seems out of their reach.

Some teens with depression eat because they feel sad. They think their favorite junk food, a heaping serving, or comfort food will make them feel better. On the other hand, eating disorders can sometimes lead to depression. If your teen isn't getting the nutrients their body needs, they can change the chemical makeup of their brain, depriving it of what it needs to function properly. This can change their mood, making them feel negative, sad, and tired, therefore leading to depression (Sander et al., 2021).

Symptoms of Eating Disorders

You can often see physical markers of an eating disorder because your teen is getting very skinny or gaining a lot of weight. Sometimes, it's hard to notice these changes until they've experienced an eating disorder for a long time. Just as it's hard to tell your children are growing taller because you see them every day and the change is subtle over time, it can be tough to see changes in their weight until it looks very drastic.

You can watch what your teen is eating for meals and see if they are getting enough. Maybe they aren't actually eating but rather moving the food around their plate until everyone else is done, and they can leave. Maybe they are skipping breakfast, and you're not sure if they eat lunch at school. Noticing these patterns can help you keep a closer eye on their weight and how their clothes fit.

Some teens with eating disorders will try to avoid eating at home completely. They might say they have to study at the library and will grab dinner while they are out. They might say friends have invited them over for dinner, or they ate something after school and aren't hungry now.

If your teen has bulimia, they might act normal when they eat meals with the family but promptly excuse themselves when dinner is over. You might listen to hear them throwing up, but they might try to mask the sounds. They might run the sink or shower while they throw up or use the bathroom.

They might start showering right after dinner to try and keep you guessing about if they are running water to cover up their vomiting or actually showering.

As with other harmful behaviors, general signs of depression and anxiety can also be symptoms of an eating disorder. You might not be able to tell yet if your teen is losing or gaining weight, but you could notice changes in their mood, energy, or interests. If you notice that they might be feeling depressed, start talking to them—even if you're unsure about them having an eating disorder. They might open up to you and tell you everything, so you can get them help, or they might feel so supported by you that they start trying to eat in a healthier manner without the need for professional intervention.

Treatment for Eating Disorders

It's important to treat eating disorders as you notice them, so your teen won't suffer from poor physical health. Not getting the right nutrients can hinder their growth and development. It can also mean their brain isn't getting everything it needs to operate properly.

If teens get treatment for their eating disorders, they should have no problem recovering and going on to live healthy lives. There are professional psychologists and psychiatrists that can help your teen identify the root of their problem. Talk therapy will help them understand what they are going through and why.

Then, the professional might invite a nutritionist to help your teen understand what they should be eating. The nutritionist can provide background knowledge that shows your teen why they need to eat certain things. They can also work out a plan to reintroduce certain foods and vitamins to your teen, so it doesn't feel overwhelming. If a teen has suffered from anorexia, for example, they are going to have trouble sitting down and eating a full meal. The nutritionist and psychologist work together to make this feat seem possible for your teen. Over time, they will feel better about eating a balanced diet until they can block their disordered thoughts about eating.

It requires parental and familial support for your teen to get past their eating disorder. Forcing them to stay at the dinner table until they finish their meal will cause them to continue having a difficult relationship with food. Understanding what they are going through and what steps they've been encouraged to take to get past these blocks will help you support them.

There is always a possibility of a relapse because your teen has experienced a strained relationship with food. They might always feel a pull to purge after eating, but just as with depression, anxiety, and other addictions, they'll learn ways to cope with these underlying desires.

SUICIDE

Suicide is when someone takes their own life on purpose. Teens might die by suicide because they feel hopeless and overwhelmed. They don't think life is ever going to get better, so they don't want to live anymore. They might be bullied to the extent where they think everyone hates them, so they might as well end their life. They might do it accidentally by overdosing on drugs or prescription pills or by drinking too much alcohol.

Teens feel a pressure to fit in with their school environment, social circles, family life, and possible future and career. They have a need to please everyone, and if they are failing at that, they might not see a point to living anymore. Teens think with an irrational mind and act impulsively, so many don't realize that suicide isn't just a solution to what they are going through now—it's a permanent change they can't take back. It influences their parents, siblings, grandparents, extended family, friends, teachers, coaches, classmates, and more.

Over 95% of people who die by suicide have a psychological disorder, with depression being the most prominent one (Cammarata, 2017). Anxiety can also push teens to this point as well as alcohol and drug abuse and a history of self-harm. Suicide is the third-leading cause of death for young people ranging from the age of 15 to 24—which, as you know now, means they are dying before their brains are fully matured (Cammarata, 2017).

Symptoms of Suicide Ideation

Knowing that your teen is thinking of suicide requires careful observations. Most teens contemplating this act try to keep it secret. They don't want anyone to talk them out of it, and they don't want to hurt anyone by letting on to what they are thinking.

Many of the symptoms of anxiety and depression can also be signs of suicide ideation as well. Your teen might be moody, withdrawn, or express sad emotions like crying or being unable to have a serious conversation with you without breaking down. They might stop participating in things they used to enjoy and in fact seem like they've lost their zeal for life. They might have trouble sleeping or sleep too much.

Teens who are thinking about suicide might not just withdraw from you and other family members but even their friends and peers. They might start conducting risky behaviors and some of the harmful behaviors previously mentioned in this chapter, like drug and alcohol abuse or cutting. They don't care about themselves anymore, so they might try to change their body or alter their mind with these substances. They also care less about their appearance and hygiene.

If your teen talks or writes about suicide, it might be a sign of something deeper than they are actually considering.

They might brush it off as a joke, but it's still something on their mind. Teens who seem like they are saying goodbye or giving away their prized possessions might be considering suicide.

You know your teen best, so you might pick up on other behaviors that are unique to them. Something might just feel off about your teen. Always talk to them about things you're noticing. It's better to talk to them about something and realize it was just a misunderstanding than to brush it off and live to regret it. If you're noticing major behavior changes in your teen, it's likely that's something wrong, anyway. It might not relate to suicide ideation, but it might be anxiety or depression, so it's still important to get help for that as well.

Suicide Prevention Measures

Talking to your teen as much as possible can help with suicide prevention. Make sure they know that they can come to you with any problem, and you'll support them without judgment. You need to actually live that way, too. Don't tell them you care and understand and then let them catch you telling a friend or family member everything they confided in you; that can break their trust in irreparable ways.

It's always better to talk to your teen about suicide and their mental health than to brush it off or think it will go away on its own. There is no proof that talking about suicide actually pushes teens to do it, so there's no harm in being open with them about your worries or patterns you've noticed.

Some teens might be relieved that you bring it up to them. They might be desperate to confide in someone who cares and could possibly understand, but they feel too alone. By bridging that gap and talking to them first, you're opening up the lines of communication. You've done the hard part of breaching the subject, so now, your teen can relax and tell you what's going on in their mind.

This is a heavy subject, so it's important that you take it seriously. Don't bring it up at the dinner table or on the drive to school. Set aside time to talk deeply with your teen, and ensure you have privacy. Make them feel comfortable, like talking in their bedroom or the living room on cozy couches. If you bring up the subject and your teen is really uncomfortable, don't push the issue. Ask them if they'd be willing to talk to someone else, like a professional who won't share all of their details with you or anyone else unless they want it to be that way.

There are a lot of emotions involved with this topic, so tread carefully. That doesn't mean you need to leave the hard stuff untouched but rather that you should be aware of what you might feel throughout the conversation. It's understandable that you'd feel sad at the thought that your teen wants to end their life, but you might be surprised to feel anger or resentment toward them as well. You might also be disappointed in yourself for letting it get this far or guilty that you didn't notice anything until now. Your teen might feel all of those emotions as well—toward themselves and toward you. It's an emotional roller coaster of a conversation, so give yourself and your teen the space to feel a wide range of emotions.

Once you bring up the subject, let your teen talk without you interrupting them. You might have follow-up questions about what they are thinking or why they feel a certain way, but you need to give them the chance to get it all out first. If they give you time to respond or ask your thoughts on what they've shared, don't diminish any of it. Don't say it doesn't sound serious—even if it doesn't. You aren't the one experiencing it, and you don't know how it feels to your teen at the moment. They might not be telling you the whole story because they are trying to see how you react to this preview first.

It's important to rephrase things, so your teen feels understood instead of projecting your own feelings into the discussion. Don't say, "I had trouble with keeping friends when I was in high school, too." Say things like, "It sounds like you're worried your friends are leaving you behind," or "It seems like you're worried about your friendships; can you tell me more about it?"

You don't want to give advice—even if you've been through something similar or feel like you have a good idea. This isn't a problem to solve for your teen. You just need to make them feel heard now. Ask them questions that keep them talking instead of yes or no questions, so you can get a better idea of what they are thinking and feeling.

It's okay to ask your teen if they are considering suicide and, if so, how serious they are about it. Ask if they've made plans. Ask when they planned to carry it out, so you know if they are in immediate danger. Ask all of these questions without judgment—you're only trying to get the information. Once you have all of this information, you'll have a better idea of what kind of professional you need to contact to help your teen, and you can give them this information if your teen doesn't want to repeat it all themselves.

Reassure your teen that you're not judging them, and you're not going to tell everyone what they've told you—you just want to keep them safe. Talk to them about methods of support, so they feel like they are taking charge of their future. You can talk to their doctor or contact a psychologist or psychiatrist. You can call a suicide hotline or take them to a treatment center. If they don't seem like they want help, you might have to force them to do so for their own safety. Don't worry if they seem to hate you for these actions; they'll appreciate it later when they are further away from the depression and suicide ideation.

IN SUMMARY

Teenagers are experiencing so many mental, physical, emotional, and social changes that they often try to find their own ways to cope.

- Teens turn to alcohol and drugs to medicate themselves. They might want to numb themselves, so they don't feel any pain. They might take uppers, so they feel energetic and perform better at school or in sports. They might drink or do drugs just to fit in with others, so they feel less alone due to their depression and anxiety.
- There are things to look for if you think your teen is abusing drugs or alcohol. Knowing the symptoms can help you talk to them and get help before they damage their health or hurt themselves or others.
- Teens also use self-harm as a way to feel things or release tension. They might cut themselves to feel in control of pain in their life. They might be so overwhelmed with the stress of their daily life that cutting themselves and caring for the wound provides a necessary distraction.
- Eating disorders are another form of control teenagers can crave. Adults direct so much of their lives that they feel empowered when they refuse food and starve themselves or binge eat and then purge the food from their bodies. Dieting and

binging without purging are other eating disorders to look out for. Eating disorders harm your teen mentally and physically.

- Suicide is a serious matter than all parents worry about but don't know how to approach. The symptoms of suicide can look like all of the signs of depression and anxiety, or it might just seem like your teen is acting different. You know them best, so if something seems strange to you, talk to them.

- Talking about suicide isn't proven to push anyone to actually do it. It's better to talk to your teen and be wrong than not talk to them and lose them. You might find that you were right, and they just needed to know that someone noticed their pain and cared enough to ask about it. Talking about suicide in specific ways can help your teen get the professional and familial support they need to move on in their life.

6

STRATEGIES TO BUILD A BETTER HOME

Your home is the foundation for your teen, so you want it to be happy, healthy, and secure. They should feel safe there and like nothing will bother them or harm them. You want to provide a space where they can be themselves, explore their possible futures, and come to you for guidance and support.

Look around your home right now. You probably decorated it to reflect your personality. Maybe your favorite color is blue, and that's why you chose a blue couch. Maybe you love coziness and comfort, and that's why you have a few extra throw pillows scattered on the furniture, so people can curl up. Your decoration style says a lot about your personality but so does the way you run your home. Do you ask people to remove their shoes when they enter the house? That says a lot about your cleanliness and that you want people to feel at home when they come inside. Do you encourage your kids to invite all their friends over, so your house is always loud and bursting with guests? That says a lot about your hospitality... and patience!

In all seriousness, people can tell a lot about you just by coming into your home. Your teen feels this as well—even though they live there, too. If you have strict rules, they will feel that tension as soon as they walk through the door after school. If you let them run wild, they might not even come home after school, instead strolling in very late because there's no curfew. This type of rule sets the tone of the house as well as influences your teen's personality.

You don't have to change your style of parenting to create a happy home for your teen. The strategies outlined in this chapter will help you build a safe space for your teen and your family to coexist, come together, and create loving relationships.

THE HAPPY HOME

A positive home environment is crucial from the newborn stage and beyond. Children need to feel like their parents are looking out for them and have their physical, mental, and emotional safety in mind. This gives them the space to explore, grow, and learn. They don't have to worry about falling down the stairs because their parents have placed baby gates, so even small children are free to explore the house and learn about themselves and their family.

A problematic home environment, on the other hand, is one where no one feels safe. Children might have access to scissors and knives. There are no baby gates, and the big dog roams free and scares the children or chews their belongings. Since the young children have no boundaries and no safety net, they learn things the hard way. These tough lessons might cause them to stop exploring because they are too worried about getting hurt. They don't feel emotionally supported because they are afraid of the unknown. They don't have the freedom to explore trial and error safely because no one is there to help them.

Parents who have a problematic home environment for their children aren't bad people. There is a lot working against people in these situations, such as poverty, maternal depression, and more. Parents juggling two or more jobs each don't have the time to be present for their children and ensure they finish their homework. They can't buy the hot new sneakers each school year and often have to rely on hand-me-downs to keep their children clothed. Poor living conditions are tough to overcome, and people raised in these homes often continue the cycle when they become adults and live on their own.

Over time, a problematic home environment presents itself in other ways. Children from these homes have trouble connecting with other people. They don't feel like they can trust others, so they are mean or hold back parts of themselves to protect their feelings. They have trouble in school because there is no structure for homework or studying and no repercussions for bad grades.

A positive home environment creates teens that are the opposite. They don't have to worry about their home life, so they are already happier than many people. They know they have a roof over their head and food on the table. They know they need to act right in school and get good grades, so their parents don't take away privileges or dock their allowance. They don't feel ashamed about inviting people over, and they are more likely to strive to create this type of home once they are on their own and again later when they are starting their own families.

THE STRATEGIES

It's one thing to understand the differences between a positive home environment and a problematic one, but how can you create a happy home for your teen? These strategies will help you implement the best for your family.

Be Present

Much of the advice about supporting your teens has been that you need to be available to them and make time for them. This is repeated constantly because it's the most important piece of advice to take away from this book. There is no alternative to being present for your children.

Kids who don't have trendy clothes and get free lunch from school can still feel safe and supported if their parents are available to them. However, if kids have all of the clothes and devices they could ever dream of, plus a private chef making them lunch, but can't talk to their parents, they aren't going to be a well-rounded, happy adult.

When you're present for your teen, you need to make sure you prioritize them when they are with you. No sneaking glances at your phone or the TV. Shut everything off, look them in the eyes, and listen to them. Don't interrupt or project your own thoughts or feelings onto what they are saying.

Be Positive

Being positive doesn't mean you have to spin everything into something good. Toxic positivity is damaging because it's not how life works. There are bad things in life, and it's important that your teen can recognize them and work past them, but you can be positive where it counts.

Show affection. Hug your teen. Kiss them even if they pull away. Cuddle with them when you're watching movies on the couch. Being available to talk and listen is another way to be positive.

Praising them, being vocally proud of them, and encouraging them when they are doing good things—and hard things—is another way to show positivity. You're showing them that you notice what they are doing and take pride in them and their accomplishments. If they try something hard and fail, you can still praise them for being brave and attempting something they didn't know if they could do.

Be a Role Model

If you're going to be proud of your teen for tackling something hard, be proud of yourself as well. Be open with your struggles and accomplishments. Show your teen that life isn't easy just because you're an adult. So many teens think that everything is easy once they are out of college or have a family of their own. Be honest about some of the problems you're having at work. Talk about being nervous for a presentation you have to give. Show them that you're a regular person with struggles, but you also empower yourself to overcome these obstacles. You're setting a good example for your teens this way. You're letting them know that they can talk about what they are facing and that you'll support them just as you tell them what's going on with you, and they support you.

Regularly talking to your teen about what's going on in your life helps them understand you as a person. You're not just an adult who feeds them breakfast and dinner and drops them off at school. You're not only a parent that scolds them when they fail a class and watches them finish their homework each night until they bring up their grades. You are a person with thoughts and feelings. You struggle and overcome. This will mean a lot to them, and they will respect you and feel more comfortable with you as a result.

Of course, being a role model extends beyond your home as well. Being kind to people who work in stores and restaurants teaches your teen a lot about how to treat others. Having valued friendships helps them realize that they can make friends for life. Driving carefully, not littering, and being considerate in public shows teens how to act—even if you're not explicitly telling them what to do. They are watching you and learning from your actions.

Declutter the House

Decluttering has become hugely popular in recent years, but you don't need to buy a whole book about it. The guidelines to declutter your house to keep it happy for teens are very simple. Basically, ensure the space feels cozy and not overbearing. Having decorations or everyday items stacked on every available surface makes it hard for your teen to feel comfortable around the house. They might worry about knocking things off of tables as they walk to their room. They might have to move a lot of stuff out of their way before they can do homework at the kitchen table or sit on the couch.

Being responsible for moving stuff out of the way, finding another place for it, and moving it back when they are done might not sound like much, but it can be a lot for a teen. They are already thinking about the homework they have to do or how they want to relax before dinner, but now, they are overwhelmed by the amount of stuff that surrounds them.

When you make an effort to declutter the house, you'll feel like it's easier to breathe. There isn't so much around that you feel stiff and need to watch how you're moving. You have more space and more freedom to take up that space. Your family can spread out in the living room and relax while you talk or watch a movie.

Decluttering is crucial in the kitchen. Having a sink full of dirty dishes looks bad, makes you feel bad, and, before long, starts to smell bad. If doing the dishes is too much for one person, make it one of your togetherness activities. You wash, and your teen can dry, or you rinse, and your teen loads the dishwasher. This way, you're both actively involved in improving the house and get to spend time together while you do it. Plus, the task always goes faster when you work together.

Living in the middle of clutter makes your brain feel over-whelmed. You'll feel stress because there is so much scattered around the house that you need to pick through when you're looking for something. Keeping your house neat and clean will help your mind feel that way as well. And if you feel such a difference, imagine how it helps your teen!

Respect Privacy

All of the previous strategies help you create the foundation of a happy home, but respecting privacy is key. If you want your teen to feel safe, then you have to give them space. You can't require them to keep their bedroom door open or allow you to read their journal. You have to trust them and give them space and freedom to explore themselves, their thoughts, and their feelings.

If you have worked to keep open lines of communication, then you shouldn't worry that your teen is hiding things from you. Well, honestly, all teens hide something from their parents, but that's normal, so you shouldn't feel the need to know everything about them. Instead, you need to know that they are safe, secure, healthy, and getting plenty of rest. They can have their own secrets and thoughts as long as it's nothing harmful.

This tip for creating a happy home isn't meant to overpower any of the previous strategies about detecting if your teen has anxiety or depression; is abusing drugs or alcohol; is harming themselves; or is thinking about suicide. In those cases, giving your teen privacy can be detrimental to their health. You don't need to hound them and force your way into their bedroom, but you need to talk openly about your worries, so they know what you're thinking and can tell you what they are up to.

Respecting the privacy of your teen refers more to letting them have friends over and not eavesdropping. Let them talk on the phone without pressing your ear to the door. If they go out with friends, don't grill them about what they did when they come home. You can be interested in their lives and what they do without finding everything out yourself. Ask them what they did with their friends or what they talked about. They'll tell you as much as they feel comfortable sharing, and they have the right to keep the rest private.

If you give your teen privacy, you're showing them that you trust them. You're not standing over them and monitoring everything they do or say. They'll feel like they can explore their personality and the world around them because you gave them a solid foundation. They learned from you as children and looked to you as their role model. You have to trust that they picked up the good lessons from you and will display that in their own behavior.

It goes without saying that privacy also includes bodily autonomy. You don't need to make your child change clothes in front of you or use the bathroom with the door open. They will want to lock their bedroom door sometimes, and that's okay and natural. You have paved the way for them to be able to talk to you about anything that's bothering them. By giving them privacy, you're showing that you respect who they are becoming as a person, and you trust them to make good decisions. Your teen will feel that trust and act accordingly.

IN SUMMARY

Creating a happy home will help your teen feel comfortable in growing and exploring their personality. They will have a safe space where they can get privacy or confide in you when needed.

- It doesn't take a major renovation to create a happy home for your teen. You have been implementing many of the strategies since the beginning of this book. Be present and positive for your teen. Be a role model and show them the actions you'd like to see them do as well.

- Decluttering the house helps declutter your mind. With fewer things taking up space around you, your whole family will feel like they have the room to spread out, relax, and be their true selves.

- Privacy is crucial for everyone but especially teens. Give them space, let them lock their bedroom door, and don't give them the third degree when they come home from a party. They'll feel the trust you have in them and act accordingly; they will still confide in you when they need to.

- Creating a happy home environment will give you a solid foundation for the strategies you'll learn in the next two chapters. They give you actionable steps for managing anxiety and depression. With the base of a happy home, you'll be free to work on other methods of coping with your teen, and they'll feel safe and secure enough to focus on themselves.

7

STRATEGIES TO BATTLE ANXIETY

L earning about anxiety in Chapter 4 gave you a broad overview of what teens experience and why, but it's important to have strategies in place, so you can battle anxiety with your teen. You'll learn how to make them feel safe around you and in your home. You'll give them strategies that can help them manage anxiety to a point where it's not crippling and unbearable. Giving your teen these skills now will prime them to handle their mental issues in a proactive way in the future as well.

It's important to realize, and ensure your teen realizes, that anxiety is common. Everyone experiences it at some point in their lives, whether they are adults or teens; seem to have it all together; are rich or poor; and so on. It's a natural emotion that you feel when you're worried or afraid of something unfamiliar to you. Knowing that everyone feels anxious can help diminish the power of this feeling. Instead of your teen worrying that they are the only one existing in this way, they can find comfort that other people deal with it as well. Those people get through and still live their lives, so your teen can do the same.

Anxiety is not a weakness. It's something everyone feels, but the secret is that you can't let it control you. Your teen will learn strategies to be the one overcoming anxiety, instead of letting anxiety steamroll them. Knowing how to manage anxiety will allow your teen to lead a happier, more empowered life.

ANXIETY THROUGH THE MAGNIFYING GLASS

Getting the facts will help your teen understand what they are going through when they feel anxious. Once they inspect anxiety through the magnifying glass, they won't feel as unsettled by the sensation they experience.

First, they should know that one in five young people experience anxiety (Young, 2019). Everyone feels anxiety differently, so there's no correct or incorrect way to be anxious. If a classmate describes their anxiety as a burst of adrenaline before they run out onto the basketball court, that's just their anxiety. Your teen might sweat and shake before taking a test and feel like their mind has gone completely blank. That is a valid form of anxiety, too. Just as every individual and personality is different, so is anxiety. Understanding that can give your teen the freedom to let their worries about anxiety go a bit. They don't have to think they are feeling something wrong because others describe anxiety differently.

Second, your teen should know that anxiety doesn't always have a cause. Many people think that anxiety must have a trigger. They spend time and effort to pinpoint their triggers, so they can work through them in therapy or try to avoid them in their daily lives, but that's not always the case. For example, your teen might experience anxiety before a big test, but they might also get anxious before they meet friends at the mall. The test and the mall aren't necessarily triggers. They might just be something high stakes or unfamiliar that makes your teen nervous. They might not even feel anxious before every social event or every test. Anxiety has no rhyme or reason, which is why it's so important to understand strategies that help you cope with it.

Third, your teen should know that having anxiety doesn't make them a bad, weak, or inferior person. You can research their favorite actors, musicians, and celebrities and find articles where they mention feeling anxiety over one thing or another. Everyone experiences anxiety at some point in their lives, and they still go on to accomplish anything they put their minds to. This will work for your teen, too. They are not weak; in fact, they are strong for facing anxiety on top of all of the other changes their bodies and minds are experiencing during puberty.

Next, make sure your teen knows that anxiety is just a feeling. Some people write off those who experience anxiety as "anxious people" as if that's the sum of who they are. That isn't accurate. Everyone experiences anxiety, but no one should be labeled as an anxious person. That's just something you feel every once in a while and shouldn't be used to describe the entirety of who your teen is as a person.

Last, reassure your teen that their brain is perfectly normal. Experiencing anxiety doesn't mean their brain is broken. It doesn't mean they can't cope with life and are shutting down when faced with a problem or something unknown. The most advanced brains still experience anxiety, so there's no reason for your teen to worry about their mental health in that manner. Their brain is functioning fine, but learning tips to cope with anxiety will only boost their brainpower and their confidence.

Before learning the strategies to cope with anxiety, make sure you understand the different types of anxiety your teen could possibly feel. Sometimes, anxiety appears as negative thoughts. Your teen might feel like others are judging them for what they are wearing, how they style their hair, or what they said aloud in class. They keep thinking about others and let that perceived judgment embarrass them until they are worried and anxious about everything in general. Thoughts are thoughts—not predictions or educated, researched facts. Let them come and go without giving them too much weight.

Other times, anxiety is excessive worries about things beyond your teen's control. It's one thing to worry about a history exam because they can make flash cards and study hard to change the possible outcome. But if they are worrying that a cough means they have lung cancer, or their paper cut will get infected, then those are excessive and not rooted in reality.

Sometimes your teen might feel anxious because of emotions like fear, feeling overwhelmed, dread, or worry. They don't know what started these feelings, but they let it escalate into anxiety and start worrying about other unrelated thoughts that enter their mind. Feelings are a surge of neurochemicals in fight-or-flight mode.

Physical symptoms can lead to anxiety as well. Your teen's heart might pound, and they feel butterflies in their stomach. They have tense muscles or shaking hands. They might feel dizzy, nauseous, or irrationally emotional.

THE STRATEGIES

Anxiety appears in different ways to different people, so not all strategies will suit your teen. Knowing the different possible types of anxiety can help you pinpoint the right strategy for your teen's anxiety. If one doesn't work, empower them to try another until they find a method that helps them the most.

Mindfulness

Mindfulness is a simple practice that can help teens feel in control of their thoughts. It's a type of exercise for the brain that helps teens acknowledge and release their thoughts to calm themselves down.

When your teen practices mindfulness, they are learning how to live in the present moment. They aren't thinking about something bad that happened in school that day or worrying about their test at the end of the week. They are only experiencing everything in the present moment.

Mindfulness helps your teen tune out things around them. For example, if your teen is playing basketball, they aren't thinking about the score or the other team. They are fully concentrating on their foul shot. They feel their feet in their shoes and see the line they need to stand on. They feel the pebbled skin of the ball against their fingertips. They take a deep breath and feel the air filling their lungs. They look at the hoop and dribble the ball before shooting. This concentration doesn't guarantee they'll make their shot, but it helps them tune out everything around them—including their negative thoughts—so they can feel completely present for the shot.

There are many benefits to practicing mindfulness. In addition to managing the feeling of anxiety, mindfulness also helps your teen stay focused on the tasks at hand. They aren't as worried about the future because they are only thinking about what's happening now. It can help them slow down and think about things before reacting impulsively. It also helps them understand self-control.

Mindfulness takes training, but it's something you can practice along with your teen. Start with a few minutes a day. Sit somewhere comfortably, but don't slouch or stretch out. Sit so that you're both aware of your bodies. Focus your attention on your breath as you inhale and exhale. As you pay attention to your normal breathing pattern, start to change your breath. Inhale to the count of four, hold your breath to the count of five, and exhale to the count of six. If you notice your thoughts straying, bring them back to your breath or change your breathing pattern.

Don't chastise yourself for wandering thoughts. It's natural and is what your brain does—even if you're attempting to focus on one thing. Try to focus on your breathing for five minutes and see how you feel. Don't keep track of how often your thoughts wander or wonder what you're going to do next. Don't think about the time, just set an alarm so you can focus on your breath completely.

After you and your teen practice this, you might find yourselves doing it when you start to feel anxious. Taking your mind off of the worries and focusing on your breath will calm you down. The breathing itself will physically calm your body, and thinking about your breath will help you realize that the anxieties aren't that important in the scheme of things. They are temporary, and your breath is constant and something to depend on.

Your teen doesn't only need to use mindfulness when they feel anxious. They can use this at any time when they feel overwhelmed or worry that their thoughts are scattered. It's a great way to center yourself and feel back in touch with your physical body and everything that matters in the moment. They can use mindfulness to help with academic work, social situations, and more.

Exercise

Experts have touted the benefits of exercise for mental health for years. When you move your body, different chemicals and hormones are activated to energize you physically and mentally. If your teen goes out for a walk or a run around the neighborhood, they are getting fresh air, leaving the constraints of their room, and getting a distraction from their daily life. But because they are moving their body, they'll get many health benefits as well.

When your teen feels anxious, they most likely already feel twitchy. Their thoughts are jumping around at a rapid pace, so they might also have trouble sitting still and calming down physically. Instead of asking them to try and calm their body down by being stagnant, encourage your teen to go out for some exercise. Moving their muscles activates chemicals that will literally calm their thoughts.

Adrenaline pushes your teen to take action. If they don't physically move, that adrenaline most likely leads to anxious thoughts. They are feeling the hormonal push of fight-or-flight mode, but they don't know what to do, so their brain is overcome with worry. If they start moving when they feel this rush of adrenaline, they'll work off the hormone and manage the stress and anxious thoughts in a positive way.

Sometimes, the neurons in your teen's brain get overactive and cause impulsive decisions, which lead to anxiety. Gamma-aminobutyric acid, or GABA, is a neurochemical that calms your brain cells (Young, 2019). However, your body can run out of GABA, so exercising boosts those levels which in turn calm your thoughts.

A quick walk or run is enough to produce GABA. If you have stairs in your house, your teen can walk or run up and down the staircase for quality exercise. They can do this any time they feel anxious, but if they have time for regular exercise five days a week, that's the best option. Regular exercise can help prevent anxious thoughts in the first place. If they can't get out and walk or run every day, try a stretching or yoga routine, so they still work their muscles. The practice of yoga also goes hand in hand with mindfulness, so your teen's anxiety is sure to melt away.

Make time to take daily walks or do yoga with your teen and see how things improve. Not only will you both produce more GABA, but you'll also have time together to talk and become closer. You'll find that you truly treasure these times.

Healthy Diet

A healthy diet is important for teens because they are growing and need nutrients to develop strong bones and muscles. Food also gives them energy to exercise, which you just learned is key to managing anxiety. Yet there's another positive way that food can help your teen manage anxiety. Certain foods benefit the brain in different ways, so eating the right diet can literally improve their brain and make them feel happier throughout the day.

Certain foods help ease anxiety because of the vitamins and nutrients they contain. Salmon has vitamin D and omega-3 fatty acids that promote brain health. They boost the levels of dopamine and serotonin, which calm the brain. Yogurt is full of healthy bacteria called probiotics. These bacteria improve your digestion and gut health, which takes a load off your mind. But science is finding links between the intestines and brain, so probiotics are showing that they improve mental health (Elliott, 2017).

Green tea contains L-theanine, an amino acid that calms your mind. Chamomile tea regulates neurotransmitters with its nutrients, which helps your body produce serotonin and dopamine. The teas also help your body produce GABA, which you get from exercise as well.

For a treat, dark chocolate is one of the best choices for your teen. If they have a strong sweet tooth, the slight bitterness of this dessert might not satisfy them, but it pays off in antioxidants and blood flow to the brain. These benefits will improve your teen's overall mood.

Other diet changes that will help your teen combat anxiety include eating protein at breakfast. You know it's the most important meal of the day, but more important than eating breakfast is *what* you eat for breakfast. Protein not only keeps your teen feeling full for a longer period but also boosts their brainpower. It raises their blood sugar, so they are able to think clearly and have enough energy to get them through until lunch.

Sugary foods and drinks might give your teen a temporary energy boost, but they aren't the best choices for a healthy diet. It's better for them to eat complex carbohydrates, like bread and oatmeal that contains whole grains. Carbs increase serotonin production, which helps their brain focus.

Drinking plenty of water also helps your teen maintain a healthy diet. It keeps their body hydrated and can also prevent overeating. Your teen should only eat when they are hungry and should eat a balanced meal each time. Feed them protein, fruits, and vegetables at each meal. Regularly eating fish that have high levels of omega-3 fatty acids will also help boost their brains over time (Sawchuk, 2017).

Quality Time

You've already learned the importance of being a good role model for your teen. Keeping the lines of communication open also gives them a feeling of support and understanding.

Therefore, it's not surprising that spending quality time together helps ease their anxiety.

Your teen will appreciate it when you put aside your work and personal demands to prioritize them. It will automatically make them feel less alone because you're showing that you're there for them.

As your child grows into a teen, they might seem like they want to be around you less. Some of this is natural because they are trying to explore their own self and see what life can be like for them once they are independent. But sometimes, it's forced upon both teens and their parents. Society makes you feel like you need to step back and leave your kid on their own, but that's not really the case.

As your teen explores what it might be like to live on their own in a few years, they need your support more than ever. They look to you to make sure they are on the right path. They still want your approval and input—even if they seem like they don't want to be around you. You might feel like your teen is pushing you away in some cases, but it's important to never let that actually happen. Don't actually take yourself out of the equation because of how they act to you. It's hard to put aside hurt feelings when you feel like your teen doesn't want to be around you or doesn't value your input, but you have to push past that and do what's best for them.

Make yourself available when they need you. Don't say you'll talk later once you turn off the computer, the TV, or put down your phone. Prioritize them, so they know they can come to you immediately with something they have to figure out right at that moment. It might feel pressing to them because they are impulsive, but if you try to disregard it as something you can deal with later, they might stop coming to you at all.

Being emotionally open to your teen will show them they can act that way with you, too. Again, it's the instance of you being the role model. Show them the behaviors you want from them. You might be surprised to find that you both enjoy sharing personal stories with each other and grow much closer. Having a close relationship with your teen not only helps you understand what they are going through now but will also help you stay close as they go to college, move away, and start a career and family of their own.

Spending quality time with your teen can work in many ways, depending on your family dynamics and schedules. Maybe you take daily walks with your teen before dinner—sometimes talking or sometimes in silence. Maybe you go out for dinner or coffee every other week. Maybe you have movie nights every Sunday and take turns choosing a movie that's meaningful to you. After you watch the film, you can talk about why you picked it, what you each liked about it, and ultimately learn a lot about each other.

Quality time doesn't have to be something you leave the house to do. You can cook dinner together once a week. You can read the same books and host an informal book discussion during dinner or after they finish their homework. There are so many ways to fit in quality time with your teen. Once you start doing it, you'll love how you naturally come together even more than you could have imagined.

Social Media Break

Taking a social media break almost goes hand in hand with spending quality time together. Too often, downtime refers to people sitting in the same room but not talking. Instead, they are each on their own devices, scrolling, liking, and commenting—in other words, interacting with everyone else except the people in the room with them.

Therefore, a social media break will bring you and your teen closer together. You'll both put away your devices and ignore the Internet. This might happen with the previously mentioned quality time. You aren't going to be on your phones when you have coffee together or watch a movie, for instance, but a healthy social media break can have an even broader reach than that.

When your teen puts aside their device and disconnects from social media, they get a chance to live their own life in real time. They aren't worried about taking pictures of what they do, so they can post it later. They aren't commenting on their friends' posts or feeling left out of what everyone else is doing. Ignorance is bliss, and in this super-connected age, that means you have to unplug to get true ignorance.

Some teens need their device and the Internet during the week for school assignments, so you might choose to have your teen do their work after school and take a technology break from dinner until the next morning. You might pick a weekend day where no devices are allowed, and the family goes on a hike, visits grandparents, does chores around the house, or attempts a craft together. Even reading books in the same room can create a sense of companionship that will help ease your teen's anxiety.

At first, a social media break might cause your teen more anxiety. They'll worry that their friends will think they are lame for not having access to the internet. They might think friends will be offended that your teen isn't liking or commenting on their posts, but once you establish this routine, your teen will start to feel free. They won't feel pressured to post, share, interact, or be consumed with what others are doing. They will be able to connect to themselves and their loved ones in real time like a different method of practicing mindfulness.

IN SUMMARY

Understanding the anxiety your teen feels is only half of the battle. You also need to know some effective ways of helping them ease these uncomfortable feelings.

- Mindfulness is a practice that helps your teen stay present in the moment. They aren't worrying about the past or future. They are only thinking about what's going on now. It helps to have them think about their breathing, so their brain has something to focus on. Then they can dismiss any other intrusive thoughts that try to cause anxiety.

- Practicing mindfulness doesn't just alleviate anxiety but also helps your teen focus their mind in other situations as well. They might use it when they feel overwhelmed at school or need to focus on a specific task, like scoring a goal during their extracurricular sports game or completing an intricate piece of art as a hobby.

- Exercise is another way to alleviate anxiety. In addition to distracting your teen by getting them out of the house and moving, exercise produces GABA— a chemical that boosts brain performance. A good workout also helps dopamine and serotonin pump through their body, which lifts their spirits and makes them feel relaxed and accomplished.

- A healthy diet helps both your teen's brain and their body. The vitamins and nutrients in balanced meals give them the energy necessary for a good workout. Certain foods are brain foods and boost neurochemicals that improve their mood and focus as well.

- Spending quality time with your teen is important in

terms of creating a strong relationship with them, but it also helps reduce their anxiety. They know you are around to talk to them and help them through any problems they are having.

- Taking a break from social media helps your teen connect with real life. They can spend time with you and the family. They can exercise and practice mindfulness. They will benefit from not staring at screens, constantly scrolling and refreshing and feeling like they are missing out on life. They'll have a chance to realize what is important to them and work on it.

- Social media breaks can be adapted to fit into your family's schedule. Whenever possible, it's a great idea for the whole family to take a break at the same time. This gives you all a chance to form deeper connections together.

8

STRATEGIES TO OVERCOME DEPRESSION

One of the most important things you can do when your teen is suffering from depression is to take it seriously. Never say or act like this is just a phase or something they'll get over in no time. Depression is serious, and if you belittle it, you'll make your teen feel worse. They might stop confiding in you. Instead, learn as much as you can about what your teen is going through. The background information in Chapter 4 provides a solid foundation about depression, but it's different for every person.

DEPRESSION AT A GLANCE

Teenagers are suffering from depression now more than ever. In the past 25 years, the rate of teen depression has increased by 70% (St. John et al., 2004). Despite the prominence of depression, only 3.2% of teens are officially diagnosed with depression (Rudlin, 2020). It's not crucial to get a diagnosis to help your teen, but it might empower both of you to take the condition seriously and get as much support as you can. Many people mistakenly think teenage depression is just mood swings, so they don't get the professional help they need.

Getting professional help for teenage depression isn't a bad thing. Just because your teen needs therapy or even medication now doesn't mean they'll need it for their whole lives. Some parents hate the idea of medicating their teen because they don't want them to get a dependence on pills, but the right professional won't allow that to happen.

A psychiatrist will get to know your teen first and then talk about different treatment options with you both. If medication seems like an option, they initially prescribe a low dose of an antidepressant to see how your teen reacts. If it doesn't help, they might increase the dose or try another type until they find the right solution.

Once your teen overcomes depression, they can step down from their antidepressants with help. They can talk to the psychiatrist about lowering their dose over time. Doing it slowly, with medical help, ensures that it's the right move. You don't want your teen to stop cold turkey and then find that they are suffering from depression once more. As they step down, they'll be able to notice if the depression comes back. Then they can stay on a lower amount of antidepressants or work back up to what they used to take. In many cases, they can keep stepping down until they aren't on medication anymore. But being on medication, even if they need it for life, is never a sign of failure. You shouldn't see it that way, and you should ensure your teen doesn't feel that way either.

THE STRATEGIES

As with anxiety, depression presents in different ways. Your teen might seem sad all of the time, or they might feel hopeless and consider suicide. Regardless of how severe their depression is, you want to implement some or all of these strategies to help them manage their issue.

Know When to Seek Help

The most important strategy for handling depression is knowing when to seek help. Some teens will cope well by being able to talk to you whenever they need. Some might prefer to keep you in the dark and confide in a professional instead. Some need medical intervention or a stay in a treatment facility if they feel suicidal. There are so many different options for depression treatment that you need to always stay aware of what's going on. As previously recommended, spending time with your teen and keeping open lines of communication is a great way to know how they feel and what they are thinking.

Treatment isn't a sign of defeat. It means both you and your teen know you're not capable of handling the issue and need someone with expertise in the subject. It's a good thing to acknowledge this and seek the right resources.

Discuss Depression

Your teen might already know what depression is, and they might already realize that they have it. Still, talking about what depression is, what it means, what it feels like, and possible treatment options opens the conversation for your teen to be better informed and feel like they can share what they are going through. If you don't really talk about emotions with your teen, they might feel like it's too hard to start talking about how bad they feel. But if you start talking about depression in a general sense, they might feel more comfortable chiming in with what they feel and what help they want from you.

During these discussions, you can get things started, but then you should sit back and listen. Give your teen the floor and let them talk about what they think and feel without asking questions or changing the subject. When they see that you're taking them seriously, they'll start sharing more, and you can get them the help they need.

As with other conversations with your teen, these discussions shouldn't be rushed. You should have time to talk and stay in a private, comfortable place, so your teen feels safe. Don't judge them based on things they say, and don't assume they mean one thing based on your personal projections. If you're unsure of what they mean, ask clarifying questions that can't be answered with a simple yes or no. Remember: You're trying to get your teen to open up to you.

Keep Your Teen Involved

As parents, it's so easy to want to take your teen's troubles and handle everything yourself. If you know they are depressed, you might be tempted to call a professional, schedule therapy sessions, and start researching possible medications on your own. It's understandable that you want to make life easy on them, but in this case, it's not the best solution.

When your teen is depressed, you want to ensure you're doing what they want within reason. If they just want you to leave them alone, you have to take steps to find some sort of option they are okay with. However, don't sign them up for group therapy if they are too shy to share personal feelings with strangers. Talking to them about treatment options and letting them tell you what they are okay with is a huge step in managing depression.

Your teen already feels like life is hopeless and nothing matters. Taking this out of their control only reinforces that belief. However, if you keep communication open and let them decide what therapy they'd like to try and what doctor they'd like to see, they start to see a light at the end of the tunnel. They understand that help is available to them. Even if you are literally making the appointments yourself, giving them the choice and input helps them see that they can change their life. In the future, if they feel this way again or hit another roadblock, they'll remember the steps you showed them to take action. They'll look for help like you did for them at this point. You are empowering them to be active in their own life and healing, and that is what a teenager with depression needs to feel.

IN SUMMARY

Teens feel depression in varying degrees, so it's important to communicate with them openly. Give them the space and freedom to tell you what they are experiencing, so you can help them manage their depression.

- There is no shame in getting professional help for depression. Many people benefit from talk therapy or medication. Depression can be a general mood disorder or a disruption of brain chemicals, and meeting with a professional will help your teen find out what they need to improve their life.
- Start discussions by defining depression. Tell your teen what it means and what it might feel like. Since you're giving them general information instead of asking them if they are depressed, they might feel more secure about opening up to you. Never express judgment during these discussions because you don't

want your teen to clam up and stop sharing
with you.

- It's tempting to want to fix everything for your teen,
but that might make them feel even more hopeless.
Give them treatment options and allow them the
freedom to choose what they think will work for
them. This empowers them to make their own
choices and also helps them see that there is always
support out there if they seek it. You're just helping
them learn this lesson that will continue to serve
them well in life.

CONCLUSION

Being a parent of a teen who has anxiety or depression is never easy. Even though they are a teen, going through all sorts of emotional and physical growth, you still want to care for them like they are your baby. The steps in this book show you how you can still be an involved parent for your teen without stepping all over their space and privacy. They will feel supported and understood but will still have the space to explore themselves and make choices in terms of treatments and moving forward in their lives.

Understanding the mind of a teen gives you a broad overview of what it's like to grow up now. Each generation has experienced different social and historical events that shape their lives. Arguably, modern teens have had some of the toughest times. There is social and political upheaval that seeps into their everyday life. They have lost out on attending school instead of having to homeschool or attend virtual school for a year or more.

The dependence on screens due to virtual school has extended to teens relying on social media to connect with others. They aren't only interacting with their friends online but also meeting strangers, exploring their identities, and learning about places and cultures they'd never have the ability to experience otherwise.

Though there are positives to social media use, there are also plenty of negative aspects. It's important to establish safe boundaries with your teen before they share information online. Some apps pull personal information and location data that can endanger your teen. It's also possible for them to share inappropriate pictures that lead to blackmail or cyberbullying. Ensuring they have a private account and don't post anything they wouldn't want you to see can keep your teen safe online.

The best thing you can do for your teen is to be a role model. Act the way you want your teen to act. Be kind to others. Think logically and research the facts before making a decision. Listen more than you talk. Always be open to communication, putting down your phone or turning off the TV when your teen comes to you. By showing them how much you care about their thoughts and feelings, you're ensuring that your teen will come to you when they are struggling.

Whether your teen regularly talks to you or not, you might have trouble identifying the signs of anxiety and depression. It can be hard to know what is a teenage mood swing and what is a more severe condition. Anxiety and depression present differently in every person, so you are the best judge of your teen's well-being. You know them best, and you know what is normal for them. If you're noticing different attitudes, behaviors, and health problems, talk to them about what's going on. Always be open and withhold judgment, so they feel confident sharing with you. If they aren't willing to talk to you, always recommend setting them up with a professional. Your teen should never feel forced to talk to you or else they'll face consequences; sometimes, talking to someone outside of the family would do best.

After learning the signs and symptoms of depression and anxiety, watch for troublesome behaviors in your teen. When teens are suffering from mental issues, they often try to self-medicate, numb the pain, or make themselves feel happy by drinking or doing drugs. They might cut themselves to distract from the pain of real life. They might strictly control what they eat or how they purge food from their bodies in order to feel like they have some sort of influence over their own life. All of these behaviors can severely damage their health, so getting professionals involved will ensure your teen doesn't hurt themselves or others.

Creating a happy home will help your teen feel safe and supported. If they have anxiety or depression, they might never feel at ease when they are at school or out in public. Your home can be their safe space. They should feel comfortable at home and know that you're looking out for them and setting boundaries for them. Yet they also need their own privacy.

Having a happy home for your teen is just one way to support them while they get through anxiety or depression. There are other strategies that you can implement to make them feel in control of their body and mind. The best thing is that most of these strategies can help you both. If you're looking for ways to be with your teen, exercising, practicing mindfulness, and cooking healthy foods together are just a few ways to spend quality time with them.

Many parents are dealing with teens who have anxiety or depression. They are struggling with alcohol and drug abuse and are trying to figure out how to reach out to teens who are harming themselves. Thinking about suicide and your child in the same sentence is never easy, but learning the strategies to talk to your suicidal teen will help you both move forward safely.

If this book helped you understand how you can relate to, listen to, and support your teen, please leave a review. Your feedback will help other parents realize that they aren't alone. It's hard enough to be a parent and harder still to parent a teen that is suffering from anxiety and depression. Your teen is your priority, but you need support as well. Telling other parents that this book helped you will show them that they can have support while they parent their own teen.

Recommending this book to other parents will help everyone save and support the next generation. Your teens are the future, and it's up to you to show them how to make good choices. This book will give you support while you lift up your teen and empower them to live their best life.

REFERENCES

American Academy of Child and Adolescent Psychiatry. (2019). *Eating disorders in teens*. Aacap.org. https://www. aacap.org/aacap/families_and_youth/facts_for_families/ FFF-Guide/Teenagers-With-Eating-Disorders-002.aspx

Arianna Huffington. (n.d.). AZQuotes.com. Retrieved December 30, 2021, from AZQuotes.com Web site: https:// www.azquotes.com/quote/638026

Bhandari, S. (2007, March 23). *Understanding eating disorders in teens*. WebMD; WebMD. https://www.webmd.com/ mental-health/eating-disorders/understanding-eating- disorders-teens

Cammarata, C. (2017). *About teen suicide (for parents)*. Kidshealth.org. https://kidshealth.org/en/ parents/suicide.html

Clarkson, A. (2017, October 9). *What's so unique about the teenage brain?* Parenthetical. https://parenthetical.wisc.edu/2017/10/09/whats-so-unique-about-the-teenage-brain/

Cottrell, S. (2020, January 2). *A year-by-year guide to the different generations and their personalities.* Parents; Parents. https://www.parents.com/parenting/better-parenting/style/generation-names-and-years-a-cheat-sheet-for-parents/

Dastagir, A. E. (2020, September 11). *More young people are dying by suicide, and experts aren't sure why.* USA Today. https://www.usatoday.com/story/news/health/2020/09/11/youth-suicide-rate-increases-cdc-report-finds/3463549001/

Divecha, D. (2017, October 20). *How teens today are different from past generations.* Greater Good. https://greatergood.berkeley.edu/article/item/how_teens_today_are_different_from_past_generations

Elliott, B. (2017, July 9). *6 foods that help reduce anxiety.* Healthline; Healthline Media. https://www.healthline.com/nutrition/6-foods-that-reduce-anxiety

Hazelden Betty Ford Foundation. (2019). *Early warning signs of teen substance use.* Hazeldenbettyford.org. https://www.hazeldenbettyford.org/articles/warning-signs-teen-substance-use

Hurley, K. (2016). *How to parent a teen that self harms.* Psycom.net - Mental Health Treatment Resource since 1986. https://www.psycom.net/parent-a-teen-that-self-harms/

Hurley, K. (2017). *Anxiety in teens: The hidden signs of teen anxiety you need to know.* PsyCom.net - Mental Health Treatment Resource since 1986. https://www.psycom.net/hidden-signs-teen-anxiety/

Iannelli, V. (2010, June 23). *Cutting and self-harm behaviors in teens.* Verywell Mind; Verywellmind. https://www.verywellmind.com/teen-cutting-and-self-harm-behaviors-2633862

International Society of Genetic Genealogy. (2016). *How long is a generation? Science provides an answer - ISOGG Wiki.* Isogg.org. https://isogg.org/wiki/How_long_is_a_generation%3F_Science_provides_an_answer

Kalin, N. H. (2021). Anxiety, depression, and suicide in youth. *American Journal of Psychiatry, 178*(4), 275–279. https://doi.org/10.1176/appi.ajp.2020.21020186

Lyness, D. (2016). *Depression (for teens) - KidsHealth.* Kidshealth.org. https://kidshealth.org/en/teens/depression.html

Lyness, D. (2017, November). *Mindfulness (for teens) - Nemours KidsHealth.* Kidshealth.org. https://kidshealth.org/en/teens/mindfulness.html

Mayo Clinic. (2018, November 16). *Teen depression - symptoms and causes.* Mayo Clinic; Mayo Clinic. https://www.mayoclinic.org/diseases-conditions/teen-depression/symptoms-causes/syc-20350985

Mayo Clinic Staff. (2019, December 21). *Teens and social media use: What's the impact?* Mayo Clinic; Mayo Clinic Staff. https://www.mayoclinic.org/healthy-lifestyle/tween-and-teen-health/in-depth/teens-and-social-media-use/art-20474437

Mental Health America. (2019). *Depression in teens | Mental Health America.* Mhanational.org. https://www.mhanational.org/depression-teens-0

National Institute on Alcohol Abuse and Alcoholism. (2019, June 26). *Alcohol facts and statistics.* National Institute of Alcohol Abuse and Alcoholism. https://www.niaaa.nih.gov/publications/brochures-and-fact-sheets/alcohol-facts-and-statistics

Ohannessian, C. M. (2014). Anxiety and substance use during adolescence. *Substance Abuse, 35*(4), 418–425. https://doi.org/10.1080/08897077.2014.953663

Pasquarelli, A., & Schultz, E. J. (2019, January 22). *Move over gen Z, generation alpha is the one to watch.* Adage.com. https://adage.com/article/cmo-strategy/move-gen-z-generation-alpha-watch/316314

Pedrelli, P., Shapero, B., Archibald, A., & Dale, C. (2016). Alcohol use and depression during adolescence and young adulthood: A summary and interpretation of mixed findings. *Current Addiction Reports*, *3*(1), 91–97. https://doi.org/10. 1007/s40429-016-0084-0

Pruitt, D. B., & American Academy of Child and Adolescent Psychiatry. (2000). *Your adolescent : Emotional, behavioral, and cognitive development from early adolescence through the teen years*. HarperCollins.

RaisingChildren.net. (2018, June 7). *Social media for children and teenagers*. Raising Children Network. https://raisingchildren.net.au/teens/entertainment-technology/digital-life/social-media

Ramunda, M. (2018, August 9). *What goes on inside the mind of a teenager?* Monica Ramunda | Rocky Mountain Counseling Services. https://monicaramundatherapy.com/what-goes-on-inside-the-mind-of-a-teenager/

ReachOut.com. (2019). *Social media and teenagers - ReachOut Parents*. Reachout.com. https://parents.au.reachout.com/skills-to-build/wellbeing/social-media-and-teenagers

Rudlin, K. (2020, April 13). *Does your teen seem depressed? Here's how to help*. Verywell Mind. https://www.verywellmind.com/initial-steps-in-helping-your-depressed-teen-2609493

Sander, J., Moessner, M., & Bauer, S. (2021). Depression, anxiety and eating disorder-related impairment: Moderators in female adolescents and young adults. *International Journal of Environmental Research and Public Health*, *18*(5), 2779. https://doi.org/10.3390/ijerph18052779

Sawchuk, C. N. (2017). *Find out how food and anxiety are linked.* Mayo Clinic; Mayo Clinic. https://www.mayoclinic. org/diseases-conditions/generalized-anxiety-disorder/ expert-answers/coping-with-anxiety/faq-20057987

Schimelpfening, N. (2021, April 18). *Is your teen's alcohol use a sign of depression?* Verywell Mind. https://www. verywellmind.com/teen-alcohol-facts-1065245

Smith, M., Robinson, L., Segal, J., & Reid, S. (2018, December 20). *Parent's guide to teen depression.* HelpGuide.org. https:// www.helpguide.org/articles/depression/parents-guide-to-teen-depression.htm

St. John, T., Leon, L., & McCulloch, A. (2004). *Lifetime impacts childhood and adolescent mental health: Understanding the life-time impacts.* https://www.mentalhealth.org.uk/sites/ default/files/lifetime_impacts.pdf

Stallard, P., Spears, M., Montgomery, A. A., Phillips, R., & Sayal, K. (2013). Self-harm in young adolescents (12–16 years): Onset and short-term continuation in a community sample. *BMC Psychiatry*, *13*(1). https://doi.org/10.1186/ 1471-244x-13-328

Substance Abuse and Mental Health Services Administration. (2014). *Results from the 2013 national survey on drug use and health: Summary of national findings.* https://www.samhsa.gov/data/sites/default/files/NSDUHresultsPDFWHTML2013/Web/NSDUHresults2013.pdf

Torres, F. (2020, October). *What is depression?* Psychiatry; American Psychiatric Association. https://www.psychiatry.org/patients-families/depression/what-is-depression

Uma Naidoo, MD. (2016, April 13). *Nutritional strategies to ease anxiety - Harvard Health Blog.* Harvard Health Blog. https://www.health.harvard.edu/blog/nutritional-strategies-to-ease-anxiety-201604139441

Wahed, S. (2019, October 8). *5 reasons teens use drugs.* Sandstone Care. https://www.sandstonecare.com/blog/5-reasons-teens-use-drugs

Wright, L. W. (n.d.). *Signs of anxiety in tweens and teens.* Www.understood.org. https://www.understood.org/articles/en/teen-anxiety-symptoms

Young, K. (2019, January 17). *Anxiety in teens - how to help a teenager deal with anxiety.* Heysigmund.com. https://www.heysigmund.com/anxiety-in-teens/

Made in United States
North Haven, CT
09 March 2023

33823860R00095